THINKING
TEACHER

How to transform your
mindset and your teaching

Dr Kulvarn Atwal

First published 2022

by John Catt Educational Ltd,
15 Riduna Park, Station Road,
Melton, Woodbridge IP12 1QT

Tel: +44 (0) 1394 389850
Email: enquiries@johncatt.com
Website: www.johncatt.com

ISBN: 978 1 915261 66 3

Set and designed by John Catt Educational Limited

To my grandmother who inspired me each and every day.

To Saran, Aneve and Rohan.

Never stop believing.

Contents

Chapter 1

Why become a Thinking Teacher?

This book is an open invitation to every teacher in the world to engage in a thoughtful, reflective personal dialogue about their motivations, thought processes, knowledge and practice. Whether you are a student teacher or have been teaching for 30 years, I invite you to consider the factors that can and will support you in a continual journey of improvement. I would like you to consider all the opportunities you currently get to step back and reflect upon both your underlying beliefs about teaching as well as your practice. My aim in writing this book is to support teachers at the beginning of their career to develop the mindset and practice to become excellent teachers. Equally, I want to enable those excellent experienced teachers to become even better. I will share my own personal experiences throughout my career as a teacher and share my perspective on why we should all become 'thinking teachers'.

My doctoral research required me to consider all the factors that impact upon teachers' engagement in professional learning in schools. I investigated the quality of the professional learning experiences in schools and the extent to which they provide formal and informal learning opportunities for teachers. I found that the learning environments for teachers in individual schools varied significantly. Through my research, I developed a framework of professional learning activities that I argued would enable school leaders to develop an expansive learning environment for staff – an environment that I entitled a 'dynamic learning community'. This dynamic learning community is defined by activities that will maximise opportunities for collaborative professional learning and enable the development of an expansive informal learning environment in schools. I published this research in my first book, *The Thinking School* (2019). In this book, I argued that the greatest influence on the quality of students' learning is the quality of teaching that they experience. And that the quality of this teaching is dependent upon the quality of teacher professional learning. The greatest responsibility for school leaders therefore, beyond safeguarding their students, must be to lead the professional learning for their staff. Through activities such as peer learning, lesson study, action research and coaching, the thinking school creates and nurtures a dynamic collaborative learning culture at the centre of a professional learning community.

On reflection, I am aware that my first book was written primarily for school leaders. A practical guide to enable them to develop and nurture an expansive learning environment for their staff team. As a colleague remarked to me at the time, 'What happens to teachers and middle leaders who want to work in a thinking school but are led by others who aren't aligned with these same principles'? My response was that it would inspire those educators to aspire to work in thinking schools or even to lead their own schools in that way in the future. I've realised now that we need to go further than that. That not only do we need to encourage the development of thinking schools and thinking leaders, even more importantly, we should aim to develop thinking teachers. If we can develop the right reflective and learning-focused mindsets with teachers early in their development, we can potentially transform the impact of our education system on all our students. Regardless of whether you aspire to be a great teacher or a great leader, you will develop the motivations, attitudes and practices that will have a powerful positive influence on all the students that you teach and all the colleagues that you work with.

'I am certain that teachers enter the profession because they want to make a positive difference to children's lives'. This is the first sentence of the book, *The Thinking School.* and I still agree with this statement. Equally, I have a few concerns about the challenges teachers continue to face in achieving this aim. I am concerned about the number of teachers that leave the profession each year. Recent research has indicated that 40% of teachers leave the profession before the end of their fourth year of teaching. I am also concerned about the performativity culture in schools that stifles teacher learning and student learning. I am concerned about the lack of quality authentic professional learning activities for teachers in schools. I am concerned about the lack of opportunities for teachers to engage in reflective practice, to take risks, to safely make mistakes. This book is written for every teacher at every level. The invitation to become a thinking teacher is to become someone who is unafraid of being creative, of taking risks and learning from mistakes. A teacher who enjoys the opportunity to use a mirror to reflect upon their practice and who actively wants to engage in a continual lifelong journey of improvement. Someone who wants to think and learn and not just accept what they have been told. Equally, qualities I believe we should seek to nurture with those that we teach.

Throughout my career I have been fascinated about becoming the best teacher that I can possibly be and considering all the activities that can support me in doing that. As a leader, I've taken this further and considered all that I can do to support those that I lead to continually improve. This excites me and there is not a day when I don't consider how I can become a better teacher or leader than I was the day before. Through this book, I will share my own journey and detail how you can develop the values, skills and tools of reflective practice to become a thinking teacher. This book is for every person who loves to teach and wants to be the best that they can be. For those who don't want to play safe and do what they have always done and are passionate about growing, learning and improving.

The journey towards becoming a thinking teacher is detailed in depth in each of the following chapters:

Chapter 1: Why become a Thinking Teacher

In this chapter I will ask you to undertake a reflective conversation with yourself. To consider your motivations and underlying values and how this influences your approach to teaching. I will demonstrate to you the importance of your own professional learning and how this can impact upon your students' learning.

Chapter 2: Developing as a Thinking Teacher

In chapter 2, we begin to consider what it feels like to be a learner in your classroom. Within the inherent complexity of your classroom, we consider ways in which to create and nurture effective conditions for learning for all your students. As a thinking teacher, we will explore ways through which you can transform your own mindset as well as the learning experiences of your students.

Chapter 3: Developing reflective practice

In chapter 3, I will outline strategies that you can deploy to support your development as a reflective practitioner. This is essential to your progression as a thinking teacher. By regularly engaging in reflective practice, it will become part of your natural engagement as a teacher and lifelong learner.

Chapter 4: Activities for Thinking Teachers

In chapter 4, I outline specific activities that thinking teachers are expected to engage in to support their professional learning. I will share my understanding and experience of participating in action research, peer learning, lesson study and appreciative enquiry.

Chapter 5: Strategies for Thinking Teachers

Chapter 5 will build upon the reflective practice discussed in chapter 3 and the activities shared in chapter 4 and ask you to consider 'how' you teach. I will invite you to consider the value of developing your understanding of assessment for learning, dialogic teaching (oracy) and metacognition to enable you to have the greatest possible impact on each of your students.

Why we need Thinking Teachers

Through the course of this book, I will present the findings of my own research as well as sharing additional relevant research with you. I will also draw upon my own personal experiences as a student and teacher, as well as my professional expectations of school leadership. My aim is to share my expertise with you to enable you to consider and crystallise your understanding of the kind of teacher you aspire to be and what you need to do to get there. I will also invite you to examine the values and motivators that underpin your practice and your desire to improve.

I completed my Postgraduate Certificate in Education (PGCE) at the University of East London in 1999 and I am happy to say that I enjoyed every minute of it! My previous experiences of education at school and university hadn't adequately reflected the ways in which I enjoy learning (although I didn't know that at the time). I enjoy questioning, debating and engaging in critical professional dialogue. I enjoy undertaking research and learning through discovery. I enjoy taking risks and actively learning from mistakes. My experiences at both primary and secondary school level did not encourage me to engage in the learning experiences that I now know and believe to be valuable. Up to this point I had always been successful academically, but I now know I had achieved this by playing safe. I have a reasonably good memory and I was relatively successful in passing written examinations dominated by the recitation of facts. The PGCE enabled me to be much more active in leading my own learning. I learned the value of engaging in deep thought and reflection in order to improve my knowledge and understanding and practice.

Despite this great learning experience, at no point did I feel completely confident and ready to be effectively teaching my own classes! Teaching is such a complex activity that I believe it is a profession that you can never completely master or conquer. This is also what makes it so exciting. You are constantly being challenged and engaged in a continual journey of improvement. This is really important to remember for all teachers. You will teach great lessons yet, equally, you will inevitably teach lessons that aren't as successful and that is ok. The value of becoming a thinking teacher is to have a deeper understanding of the factors that will enable you to become more consistent in teaching really successful lessons.

In performativity cultures that I have experienced, teachers have been expected to teach these one-off 'outstanding' lessons. I will discuss later how these cultures and expectations stifle creativity and improvement. The teaching of a 'perfect' lesson does not mean it will be plain sailing from now on in, and a disappointing lesson should not be seen as the end of the world either.

It is important to remember this when you first start teaching. As a newly qualified teacher (NQT), I remember being completely petrified in the days and weeks before I took responsibility for my first class in the autumn of 1999 in a primary school in the London Borough of Newham. I remember staring at the door of my classroom – at the list of names of children assigned to my year 5 and year 6 (ages 9 to 11) split class. I remember focusing on the name at the top, a girl called Stacey. My immediate thoughts were that surely the school had made an almighty mistake. Had the headteacher at the school lost her mind? Did they realise that I did not know what I was doing? How could the school leave me alone with sole responsibility for the learning of 30 children for an entire year? How would I survive now that I would no longer receive guidance and support from my university tutors? And most importantly, did Stacey's parents realise what they were letting themselves in for?

Imposter syndrome does not even begin to tell the story of how I was feeling. I realised that there were two overriding feelings that were dominating my thoughts and fuelling my anxieties. Firstly, I was concerned that my success, to date, as a teacher was due to the professional learning activities that I had engaged in during my university course. I was concerned about what I would now do without these activities to support me. Secondly, I considered myself to be an imposter – I had never, up to that point, seen a primary school teacher that either looked like me or spoke like me. I felt like I was selling my students short. I was a young working class Asian British male and my personal experiences up to that point had led me to the association that primary school teachers were predominantly white middle class women.

To a certain extent, my feelings of imposter syndrome have never ever completely disappeared during my career – I have questioned my suitability and capability each time I have faced a new role or new challenge. I have, however, used these feelings in a positive way to enable me to remain humble and to fuel my continual drive to be the best version of myself that I can be and to never stop reflecting and learning. This also supported the first major decision I made as a NQT and that was to begin my MA in Primary Education Practice. I realised that what I had enjoyed doing most during my PGCE was engaging in reflective practice and action research. I felt strongly that the MA would enable me to continue this learning journey. That by engaging in reading, reflective practice and a cycle of ongoing enquiry and action research, I could continue to improve my practice and become the best teacher that I could be. This is at the heart of the thinking teacher – a practitioner who engages in a daily cycle of reflective practice to trial changes to make improvements to practice. The aim of this book is to enable you to also develop the mindset, skills and tools to become a thinking teacher.

You may question the need for thinking teachers? We need thinking teachers because we continue to see considerable disparities between the quality of teaching in our classrooms and, consequently, the quality of our students' learning experiences. This disparity is inherently unfair and has a greater negative impact on our most vulnerable and disadvantaged students. Returning to that first class I taught in 1999, I was shocked to find that there were students in that class who couldn't read. And these individual children had been born in England and had English as their first language. I was shocked to see that children could proceed through our schooling system and get to the age of ten and have such low literacy and numeracy skills. From my perspective, I believed that this could only have happened through a combination of low expectations and ineffective teaching. I do believe that the overall quality of teaching in our schools has improved considerably over the subsequent 20 years. However, we continue to see the negative impact of the combination of low expectations and ineffective teaching upon groups of students.

We need thinking teachers because I quickly realised that the best teachers in the school and those that made the greatest positive difference to the students in their care were the teachers who were reflective, self-motivated and optimistic in their outlook. They built positive nurturing relationships with their students and set high expectations for their behaviour and their learning. I compared this to other teachers I met who were negative, pessimistic, demotivated and clearly set limitations on what they thought their students could achieve. I made the decision in my first year to become a thinking teacher. To become a teacher who would constantly seek to improve and develop. I also made it my career goal to consider how I could create an environment in a school in which the structures and cultures in place would encourage all teachers within this thinking school to be thinking teachers. In this first chapter, I will revisit the key activities that you are expected to engage in within this dynamic learning community of thinking teachers.

The Thinking School

In *The Thinking School* (2019), I discussed the importance of the learning environment in schools in impacting upon the quality of teacher learning experiences. I believe there is great disparity in schools in terms of their effectiveness in promoting professional learning and how this impacts on the opportunities for teachers to learn from and with their colleagues. Researchers (Evans et al, 2006; Billet, 2006; Kraft and Papay, 2016) have discussed the individuality of school environments and the extent to which the hidden workplace curriculum impacts upon the richness and quality of learning that occurs outside of typical formal teacher learning opportunities made available. In the UK, we would refer to the five designated training days and the one hour per week staff meeting after school as formal professional learning opportunities.

By focusing solely on these formally designated times made available for teachers, we can miss the opportunities to create a really powerful dynamic learning environment in our schools. Having just experienced a full, challenging day of teaching in the classroom, is a one-hour staff meeting at the end of the school day really the best time for a teacher to focus on learning? Instead, as a school leader, I am arguing for the creation of an expansive learning environment that enables teachers to learn continuously throughout the working week. And that fundamental and central to the role of a teacher is the expectation that we are constantly thinking, reflecting and learning throughout the school week – both formally and informally. In their review of the impact of informal learning at work, Fuller et al (2005) detailed how the workplace offers opportunities for workers to learn alongside colleagues and through the undertaking of their roles. My argument is that just through fulfilling the role of a teacher, you will be engaging in formal and informal learning activities. For teacher professional learning to be as successful as possible, we need to make it as easy and accessible as possible for teachers to engage in.

The environment in your school will influence the extent to which you experience the range of learning opportunities that are ideal for your personal and professional development as a thinking teacher. However, as teachers, we cannot simply wait for the development of such schools and I have written this book specifically for teachers to encourage them to positively influence the learning environment that they are in. Your development as a teacher cannot be down to potluck and regardless of the environment you are in, I am encouraging you to take charge of your own learning. In this section, I present the findings of my research and the development of this dynamic learning community – a range of formal learning activities for schools to implement and teachers to engage in, that will directly influence the quality of their informal learning. I describe it as 'dynamic' because I believe that the model has a dynamic effect on the attitudes and dispositions of the participant teachers, particularly those new to the profession. Additionally, as the community grows, it has a dynamic effect in reproducing thinking teachers within the model. These teachers become leaders leading the very same learning activities that they engaged in with the new teachers that join the school.

However, the development of this learning community is dependent on school leaders. They are responsible for making the decisions in relation to teacher professional development. This book is a rallying call to teachers to take responsibility to drive their own learning and positively influence the school learning environment from the ground up. To lead your own learning within the parameters and limitations of your professional learning environment. The ultimate aim is to become the teacher and leader in the classroom and beyond that you truly want to be. If we accept that the greatest factor to impact on the quality of students' learning in schools is the quality of teaching, we must equally accept the significance and power of authentically strong collaborative teacher professional learning activities.

In her 2011 book, *Student-Centred Leadership*, Viviane Robinson detailed five leadership dimensions and calculated their individual impacts upon student outcomes. Although her research focused on school leadership, Robinson shared that the leadership of teacher learning and development had twice as great an effect on student outcomes than any of the other dimensions. If I relate this to teachers in classrooms, the greatest factor you should focus on to improve your students' outcomes is your own professional learning and development. I discussed earlier that I am focused on becoming a better teacher each and every day and that is what I would like you to really focus on too. Let's reflect on this by considering a research study from Kraft and Papay (2016).

This study discussed how newly qualified (NQTs) and early career teachers (ECTs) were less effective in their teaching than their more experienced peers. That would certainly make sense; more experienced teachers would be more skilled than those newly entering the profession. They also discussed that, on average, ECTs will make rapid progress in their effectiveness as teachers during the first few years of their career. This also makes sense as ECTs certainly have lots still to learn when they first qualify. Now, I don't think many people would disagree with this hypothesis, would they? There certainly may be some ECTs who have a range of fantastic skills on entry to the profession. However, taking into consideration the complexity of the job, we would expect more experienced teachers to have a wider skillset, to reflect their greater experience. I recall how, during my first year of teaching, activities such as planning and assessment seemed to take me far longer than many of my more experienced colleagues. I was in awe of the skills and knowledge that more experienced colleagues demonstrated on a daily basis – they made teaching look effortless. However, even at that early stage, I could see that teachers differed dramatically in terms of their effectiveness, motivations and dispositions, regardless of their relative experience.

The reason that I have referred to this research paper is because their findings reflect the assertion that these rapid gains in effectiveness in these first few years are, on average, not sustained. They argue that there is significant variation between schools, both in terms of teacher effectiveness and the pace of their improvement. They argue that some teachers improved two to three times faster and continued these rapid gains through their first ten years in the job. I would argue that the reason these teachers make these improvements, in comparison to others, is that they are engaging in reflective expansive professional learning activities. Their attitudes and dispositions to learning are different. Essentially, they are thinking teachers and that is what I am inviting you to become. You cannot rely solely on the environment in your school to facilitate your professional learning; you must take responsibility and drive this for yourself.

Kraft and Papay (2016) also argue that the school environment is significant in influencing the quality of teacher learning and consequently, the extent to which teachers continue to improve throughout their careers. They relate this effect to the relationships among colleagues and a positive school culture. Regardless of the culture and even in the absence of working in a thinking school, I am asking you as thinking teachers to develop this positive culture for yourself and engage in collaborative learning activities within your own teams and in your year group/departments and schools.

Central to the development of thinking teachers and thinking schools is the professional learning environments that we engage in. We can create a dynamic learning community in which a strong focus on teacher learning will have a powerful positive impact on our students' learning outcomes (Ultimately the transformation of schools into thinking schools will support the learning and retention of staff as well as the learning of students). Higher-achieving schools have a greater capacity to support teacher professional learning because of a greater emphasis on the development of conditions that promote social capital, such as trust, opportunities for collaboration and networking. That is why it is so important for you to develop good relationships with your colleagues, based on mutual challenge and trust. I have always felt that the quality of working relationships in a year group/school can make a real positive difference to its effectiveness. It is not the people within a school that make the difference; it's the relationships between them that matters most. By 'relationship' I am referring to the quality of those working relationships and the subsequent focus on student outcomes. As a thinking teacher, therefore, I will demonstrate the importance to you of developing strong professional learning relationships with your colleagues – something I didn't always see the value of when I was an early career teacher!

The following table includes a reproduction of the key findings of my doctoral research in terms of the development of a conceptual framework of professional learning activities – the dynamic learning community. There are key features within this model that, as thinking teachers, I would like you to take every possible opportunity to engage in. Participation within these activities, preferably in collaboration with your colleagues, will enable you to experience an environment in which each day presents learning opportunities, and you will be constantly thinking, reflecting, learning and improving. In table 1, I have charted the key factors that the findings from my research and practice suggest will support teacher professional learning.

The dynamic learning community

Formal learning activities	Informal learning outcomes
1. Research based learning – formal opportunities made available to think creatively and trial changes to practice.	1. Reflective practice is seen by teachers as part of their role – they naturally begin to question their own practice and take risks.
2. Opportunities for teachers to select their own focus for professional learning, matched to their individual learning needs.	2. Teachers become highly motivated and they develop a personal drive for their continual learning.
3. Teacher learning is related to children's learning needs and their day-to-day practice.	3. Professional learning and dialogue between staff will focus directly on students' learning and outcomes.
4. Opportunities to coach and be coached.	4. Importance for staff to feel valued and work within a culture of high trust and high challenge. They become more solution focused.
5. Formal opportunities that support collaborative learning: collaborative planning; opportunities to work in different groups; peer learning and lesson study; modelling of practice.	5. Activities that then support informal collaborative learning through professional dialogue amongst staff. Learning focused leaders model learning behaviours and mindsets.

Formal learning activities	Informal learning outcomes
6. Non-judgemental lesson observations focused on professional collaborative learning.	6. Learning focused evaluations of teaching and learning take place informally in a safe, supportive and collaborative learning environment.
7. Time made available for formal learning opportunities as part of role of teacher e.g. to conduct research.	7. Time made available for informal learning opportunities e.g. collaborative planning.
8. Intellectually challenging professional learning opportunities.	8. Workplace is seen as a place where staff learning is as important as children's learning.

Table 1: The dynamic learning community

I have to remind myself that this book is written for teachers and not school leaders. I am sharing the model because it reflects the findings of my research and reflects what I feel leaders should implement to create a really expansive learning environment in our schools. I'm sharing it with you for two reasons. Firstly, because I want you to consider the opportunities currently available to you to engage in the learning activities described in the table, and to urge you to do everything within your power to create those opportunities for yourself if necessary. Secondly, you may be considering leadership opportunities in the future and it is always important to consider the type of school you want to work in and potentially, the type of school that you may want to be leading in in the future.

In *The Thinking School*, I argued that through the effective implementation of the eight formal learning activities, there will be an associated dynamic effect in promoting the development of informal learning across the school. These informal learning activities will then impact positively upon teachers' attitudes and dispositions to their own and others' learning within the school. The central premise of the thinking school is that we are developing a community of learners who are continually evaluating their practice within an ongoing cycle of collaborative improvement. However, this book is about starting from the teacher rather than the school leader. I believe that I am currently working in a thinking school that I have been leading for over ten years.

However, I am also aware that the learning environment in this school is not typically reflected in the vast majority of schools. Through my career I developed the skills of being a thinking teacher long before I became a thinking leader. This book is about sharing my experiences and expertise with you in order for you to do the same.

Values-led teaching

I believe that it is imperative that all teachers consider their values and how these values inform and influence our actions both in the classroom and beyond. One aspect of being a thinking teacher is to constantly evaluate our core values and how these influence our decision making. For example, we may think that we work really hard and genuinely want the best for every student that we teach. However, we should also take time to consider our subconscious thinking. Do we genuinely hold the same high expectations for every student that we teach? Do we genuinely believe that through hard work, perseverance and great teaching, that every student can achieve? This can be challenging when, particularly in the UK, we begin to judge and group students according to ability as soon as they enter school. There is a strong tendency in our schools to have a fixed mindset about students' learning and their potential achievements. Consider the fact that it is common practice for us to group and stream students according to their current attainment and to routinely label them as 'high ability' or 'low ability'. It is commonplace to hear teachers refer to students as 'my highers' or 'my lowers'. A question for you: we wouldn't dare to group trainee teachers or qualified teachers during professional learning meetings in terms of 'higher ability' or 'lower ability' would we? Why? Because it wouldn't be good for their self-esteem and our thinking is that through engagement in the right learning activities, they can all learn the skills to be effective teachers. So why are we so quick to label our students and what is the impact upon their learning progress and outcomes? Once you have internalised that you are a low ability maths student, it is difficult to break that self-perception. I am sure that many of you reading this book will describe yourself as 'not very good at maths'. Consider the extent to which you feel this way, is it because you have the requisite 'maths chromosome' missing or because you weren't taught very well at school?

In my first year of teaching, I worked really hard and I felt that I had a really positive impact on the students in my class. I felt that all the students progressed really well in their learning. However, on reflection, I am now aware that I should have had higher expectations for those students' attainment and progress. I would argue that the quality of writing produced by the five best writers in that particular class is now matched by up to twenty-five of the thirty children that leave a year 6 classroom in the school in which I have been headteacher (my actual title is head learning leader). If someone had suggested to me at the time that I should hold higher expectations for these students' writing skills, I may have told them that we were being unrealistic. I now realise that I was subconsciously setting low expectations for some students. I have since learned that all students have the capability to surprise you and that I should set no limitations as to which students in the class are capable of achieving. I also learned that, as a thinking teacher, I should be restless in my teaching, constantly trying to ensure that I am drawing on the latest research findings to continually improve my practice and the impact I have on the students I teach.

For ease of reference, I will refer to student teachers, newly qualified teachers (NQTs), recently qualified teachers (RQTs), and indeed anyone aspiring to be a teacher, as early career teachers (ECTs). Whenever I am working with ECTs, I always begin by asking them to reflect upon their values. I do this to enable them to consider their 'why' – why they want to teach and what values and dispositions will continue to drive and motivate them in what is an extremely challenging and complex profession. I ask them to consider the following questions:

- What do you believe in?
- What kind of teacher do you want to be?
- What is your vision of a great teacher?
- What values does this person hold?
- What is your vision of a great school?

Kanter (1977) has discussed the extent to which leading organisations use their values and core beliefs as a strategic guidance system. I believe in the importance of humility as a teacher and school leader – we are there to serve our students. By continually reflecting upon these questions and considering our values, we are refining and developing our core beliefs. It is important to continually have these self-reflective conversations to understand how these core beliefs impact upon our actions in the classroom, both positively and negatively. When you are teaching your class, you are the leader of a complex ecosystem. Be aware that you are the lead learner in the classroom and that you are modelling the learning behaviours that you equally want to develop in your students. Remember that your students will internalise the values that you hold. At a simple level, if you keep your desk tidy, you are demonstrating to your students the value of having a tidy desk/classroom. They will then be more likely to hold those values themselves. At a more complex level, if you are open, trusting, inclusive and passionate about the learning outcomes of your students, they are equally more likely to be motivated and collaborative in their learning and open and trusting with you.

I discussed earlier that I wasn't a great student myself and didn't really engage as productively as I could have done in the classroom until my PGCE. I was always relatively successful at school, but I wasn't as self-motivated and engaged as I could and should have been. What I am attempting to say is that the way in which I was taught by many of my teachers didn't really suit me. I felt that too often, I was a passive recipient in the classroom. This is because I like to talk, I like to critique, I like to debate and engage in collaborative social learning with others. I recently read through a number of my old secondary school reports. Although I was achieving relatively well, the reports are dominated by negative comments (in my opinion):

'Too chatty'.

'Lack of focus'.

'Needs to apply himself more'.

'Inattentive'.

'Works only with constant supervision'.

'Much greater effort needed'.

And my personal favourite from my form tutor in year 7 and year 8: *'He does persistently chatter at times, which appears to hinder his progress'.*

If you read these comments on a school report and didn't know this student, what would be your first impressions of them as a learner? Would your first impression be that this would be the report of a lower-attaining student? Would you expect this student to go on to complete a doctorate?

The reason I am sharing this, apart from (hopefully) making you smile, is the fact that I never felt my teachers believed in me. They did not give me the confidence to believe that through effort and perseverance, I could succeed.

As a teacher, the most important 'subject knowledge' I need to have is knowledge of the students that I teach. The foundation of great teaching is the formation of strong learning relationships with the students that you are teaching – to understand exactly where they are in their learning as well as their motivators. I strongly feel that I need to teach my students in the way that they need to learn rather than being fixed in my approach. Every student is unique and that is something that makes teaching such an exciting job. I recently met two of my former students for the first time since they left my class aged 11 – one is now aged 28 and the other is 22. Both were so happy to see me and explained to me the positive difference that I had made in their lives. There were two factors that mattered most to them. Firstly, the fact that I built such a positive relationship with them – they could feel that I genuinely cared about them as people and students. Secondly, they realised that I believed in them, and this gave them the self-confidence to see themselves as learners.

I am sharing this because I believe that, as teachers, we can never have a neutral impact on our students. We either make a positive difference or a negative one. One core value I have is to remember the importance that I hold to each and every student I teach in shaping their lives, particularly in their relationship with the learning process. This is a powerful responsibility that cannot be underestimated. I have the power to enable these students to build self-confidence and to develop the skills of lifelong learners. Equally, I also have the power to destroy their confidence. Your students will always remember you so consider carefully what you want them to remember you for and the impact that you would like to have.

You may well be able to teach effectively without building strong positive relationships with your students. However, I would argue that the better you know and understand your students, the more effective you can be. Values-led teaching is about understanding the impact you are having on the whole child. Those two students couldn't necessarily remember the learning intentions that I taught them, but they could vividly remember how much I cared and how I made them feel. I was a positive influence on them as people as well as learners and I know that this is important to me because it represents one of my core values. Your values inform your actions and those actions are modelling your expectations for those you lead, both staff and students. I am open as a school leader in sharing with the staff team my belief in the importance of developing students that are good readers, writers, mathematicians, scientists. Even more importantly, they also need to be good people and we have a pivotal role to play in that.

So, take time to consider your values, your core beliefs, your motivations, your 'why', and how this will influence your actions in the classroom. As a thinking teacher, this is about reflecting deeply upon your values and beliefs and considering both how these values influence your teaching and what you may want to reconsider to improve your teaching. Through the course of this book, I will share ways in which you can learn to do that. Becoming a thinking teacher is about challenging yourself and learning to maintain your strengths and actively working to improve your areas for development. One of the reasons I began my MA as a NQT was because I recognised that I was a better teacher of maths than I was of English. To be the teacher I wanted to be and to have the impact I wanted to have, I was honest with myself and recognised that I needed to improve my English teaching (amongst several other areas!). My first module on the MA was, therefore, Primary Literacy in Practice and I was able to learn in greater detail the various processes children engage in when learning to read. During the first MA session, each participant was asked in turn to explain their motivations to undertake a MA, and the stock answer given was to get a promotion or to become a deputy head. I explained that I wasn't really interested in the qualification or even future job aspirations. My motivations were straightforward: I just wanted to become a better teacher. Even now, every ECT I work with is encouraged and supported to begin a MA in their first year of teaching.

Your values are important to you as a teacher because you are shaping and influencing the lives of the students that you teach. It's different from working in a factory or on a building site because our values influence our attitudes towards children and young people's learning. In the next section I will detail how our workplace and life experiences influence our individual attitudes and dispositions to our learning. I will also argue that you can take charge of your own professional learning to support you to develop and maintain those positive attitudes and dispositions.

Individual dispositions to learning

Teachers differ in the extent to which they are motivated to engage in their own professional learning. Returning to my formative years as a teacher, I was fascinated by these apparent disparities and the subsequent range of learning experiences felt by students and the extent to which they were dependent on which teacher they were with. Whereas some teachers were reflective, enthusiastic and self-motivated, others were the opposite. We do have to acknowledge that, as teachers, we are also limited by the professional learning environment in which we are working in, particularly in relation to the range of professional learning opportunities on offer to us. Returning to Kraft and Papay's (2016) study, they made it clear that school contexts matter greatly to teachers and, consequently, their students; this is reflected strongly in my own research. My determination in writing this book is to encourage teachers to take greater responsibility for their own professional learning. Whilst doing so, you can also positively influence the professional learning environment around you.

School culture is significant because for thinking teachers to be successful, they need to be encouraged to be successful, they need opportunities to be creative, take risks, make mistakes and trial changes to their practice. Take for example judgemental high-stakes graded lesson observations. Throughout my career as a teacher, until I became a deputy headteacher and ended the practice, individual lesson observations were used to make judgements about teachers and their effectiveness. Typically, a senior leader would visit your classroom and watch your lesson, making notes as they did so. They would then proceed to make a judgement of your lesson, usually according to a 4-point grading scale. Most teachers would spend considerable amounts of time and energy in preparing for these 'show lessons'. I'm sure there was some value in these lesson observations and titbits of advice and recommendations would be gratefully received. But usually, the end of the observation for the teacher and associated feedback would be accompanied by a huge sigh of relief. A feeling of, 'At least I don't need to do that again for a while'. All teachers wanted to know was their judgement and the hope that they wouldn't be judged as 'inadequate' or 'requiring improvement'. I would argue that lesson observations in this form were mainly about 'performing' for the observer rather than an expansive professional 'learning' opportunity. From my perspective, the process actually stifled my professional learning as a teacher and I improved despite these observations rather than because of them. I improved when I wasn't being observed.

This was because I didn't see these lessons as genuine opportunities to engage in professional dialogue about the impact of my teaching on my students. It was more of a tick box exercise. You cannot define my impact as a teacher over the course of a year on a single one-off lesson observation of 30 minutes. As an early career teacher, I have explained that I was consciously aware of both my strengths and the areas of my practice that I needed to develop. As a thinking teacher, it is imperative that we are approaching our teaching in this way. We cannot afford to wait for these 'lesson observations' to improve. When I was being observed within this performativity culture, therefore, I ensured that I taught those lessons that I knew I was already good at – I was good at teaching maths, PE, personal, social and health education (PSHE) for example, and I was aware that I had great relationships with the students so I could be creative in my use of the classroom, incorporating drama and role-play seamlessly to 'wow' the observers! But these 'performances' did not help me to learn and improve as a teacher and weren't necessarily reflective of the various learning experiences that we would engage in during the week. What I needed to enable me to grow and develop was to be observed teaching science, art, music, because these were my areas for development.

Positive individual dispositions to our own professional learning include the need to drive and direct our own professional learning. What I was doing in the example presented was playing it safe, sharing only my strengths, and actively hiding my areas for development. The typical performativity culture in most schools encourages many teachers to do exactly the same and leads to the rapid early improvement of teachers in their first two years and their improvement potentially flattening out from their third year onwards. We can stick to what we know and begin to play safe and even resistant to change. Thinking teachers will do their best to avoid this by constantly looking outwards, engaging in research and being creative in trying to continually improve their practice. And you may have to do this despite the limitations of your professional learning environment. Consider the lesson observations that you currently engage in and the extent to which they impact positively upon your professional learning. How brave and innovative are you prepared to be during these lessons and to what extent do you use them as really powerful professional learning opportunities. To take those risks, there needs to be a high degree of trust between the observer and the observed. As a school we have always engaged in non-judgemental lesson observations. Instead, we focus on peer learning and lesson studies as starting points for deep reflection and professional dialogue in which the experience is a powerful and dynamic learning opportunity for all involved.

Within my research, I used the term individual dispositions to learning to demonstrate that individual teachers have agency in the extent to which they engage in the learning opportunities on offer in the workplace. As a school leader, particularly when taking on a new school, I am fully aware that some teachers will be highly self-motivated and enthusiastic to engage in the learning opportunities that I promote, such as peer learning, lesson study, coaching, action research. Equally, I know that others may be less enthusiastic. For example, although I encourage every teacher to undertake a master's degree, I cannot expect all teachers to instinctively want to engage in research. Some may not have the time to devote to further study or may be apprehensive about writing assignments for example. However, it is my job to make engagement in research as easy and accessible as possible for teachers to participate.

These differing levels of motivation and engagement may also indicate differences in individual dispositions to learning. These dispositions are influenced by both your life histories and your work histories. Many of the dispositions are developed during your formative years in the classroom. Some experienced teachers have chosen not to engage as enthusiastically in the professional learning opportunities I have offered simply because they felt that they didn't need to. They may have considered themselves as an established teacher and did not feel the need to engage in further research. I would encourage you to actively take responsibility for your own learning early in your career and nurture positive individual dispositions to your own professional learning and development. If, like me, you believe that teaching is a profession in which we are continually learning, growing and developing, then let's start as we mean to go on. As thinking teachers, take every possible opportunity in the workplace to reflect, question and critique your own practice. Take opportunities to engage in professional dialogue and collaborative learning with your colleagues.

Some teachers are unwilling to take risks because they are uncomfortable with change. I would urge you to embrace making changes to your practice in a positive way and as an essential part of your role as a teacher. The reason why many teachers are reluctant is that, by having to make changes to their practice, it somehow implies that what we were doing before was wrong, and the resulting self-reflection that we may have let our former students down. This is because we work within a caring profession, involved in moulding and shaping the lives of those we teach, it is sometimes difficult to accept that we could have somehow done better. I look back to that first class I taught and accept that I could have done better. Not because I didn't work hard or try my best; I am confident that I did my best with the tools, knowledge and understanding of teaching I had at the time. However, I am also aware that, as a profession, we should be expected to continually learn and improve. We should now know more about the craft of teaching than was available to me in my first year. Equally, consider the improvements in technology available to support students' learning. I also expect my knowledge and understanding of effective teaching to continue to improve in the years to come.

This chapter is designed to enable you to consider your values and how these influence your dispositions and attitudes to your own learning and your actions in the classroom. I have encouraged you to take creative risks with your learning and practice and to not view making changes to your practice as an uncomfortable process. This is a lot easier when you are working within a school in which collaborative professional learning and research-based practice is encouraged. However, I've spoken about values because I want you to aspire to become the teacher that you want to be, regardless of the environment within which you are currently working. As an individual, you can influence the quality of the learning environment in your school. I was discouraged by senior leaders in my first school to begin my MA in my first year of teaching. I was told that it was more appropriate for experienced teachers to undertake a MA and that I would struggle to cope in my NQT year. So, I undertook the MA in secret. I was clear in my appreciation of the value – to both me and my development as a teacher – in engaging with research. My individual dispositions to learning meant that I had to decide in the best interests of myself and the students in my class. And I am very glad that I did!

In the next section, I define this values-based approach as learning-focused teaching.

Learning-focused teaching

Through my research I developed the concept of learning-focused leadership and I believe it enables me to remain grounded and focused on my capacity as a head learning leader. Learning-focused leadership is primarily about ensuring that as a leader, you are focused on your own learning and the need to consistently grow and develop. Additionally, it is about ensuring that every decision you make and every action you take is considered in terms of its impact upon your students' learning outcomes. As a school leader, I view every single member of staff as a leader, and I view our teachers to be the most important people in our school, after the students. This is because they are in the position of making the greatest difference to our students' learning. They are the ones on the front line, making thousands of decisions every day that will impact upon how our students feel, what they do and how much they learn. As I discussed earlier, the greatest single influence on the quality of students' learning in schools is the quality of teaching. That is why my focus as a leader is on creating an environment in which teachers can engage in expansive professional learning activities, in a climate which enables them to be the best that they can be. In our school, our teachers are called class leaders. They are responsible for leading their own learning, the learning of their colleagues, and crucially, the learning of their students. There is no more important leadership role in a school than the leadership of a class of students and as school leaders, it is our aim to develop the structures and cultures in our school that encourage learning-focused teaching for all.

There are two aspects to your development as a learning-focused teacher. Firstly, you are continually focused on your own learning and development as a teacher. Being learning-focused means that you are constantly curious and restless about your practice, reflecting on your planning and decision making in light of relevant findings and research. You take every opportunity to collaborate and learn from and with your colleagues. A learning-focused teacher is hungry to continually gain knowledge and skills to be the best teacher that they can be. In my first year of teaching, my ambition was to become the best teacher in the world – not because I saw it as a realistic and measurable goal, I simply wanted to get the very best out of myself. To this day, I remain genuinely excited about introducing changes to my practice in my continual journey of improvement. Learning-focused teachers engage with literature and undertake research in their own classrooms. They collaborate with colleagues within and beyond their own school; they are innovative and creative, unafraid of taking risks and making changes to their practice.

Secondly, learning-focused teachers are focused on the 'learning outcomes' of the students that they are teaching. This may sound obvious and central to the role of the teacher. However, it is also about analysing every decision you make and every action you take in terms of the direct impact on the learning outcomes of every student you teach. You may be surprised at the number of decisions we make in school on any given day that are not considered in the best interests of our students. In fact, I would argue that in many low performing schools, decisions are often made because they suit the needs of the adults in the institution rather than the students. This is an observation more than a criticism. I am arguing that thinking teachers need to be open to reflecting upon and challenging decisions that are made at a whole school level. Particularly if you feel strongly that what you may be being asked to do is not in the best interests of your students. High performing schools nurture a culture of high trust and high challenge, in the best interests of their students.

Every decision you make as a learning-focused teacher is analysed in terms of its impact on your students' learning – not only in terms of academic learning and progress but also in terms of their personal, social, emotional and moral development. By continually asking yourself this you will develop a very positive habit of ensuring that you constantly maintain your focus on the fact that your actions are directly related to your students' learning experiences. This will also mean that you will be unafraid to deviate from your planning if necessary, or teaching a lesson again because it didn't work out the first time. I fondly remember a time when two colleagues and I engaged in a peer learning observation of an English lesson. We all noticed that the children were not as motivated and engaged in the core text as we would have expected them to be. We were also aware that the class leader in question had put a great deal of effort and energy into producing a detailed medium term curriculum plan with this particular text at its centre. The easy thing to do would have been to continue with the plan because of the time and effort it had taken to produce it, but would this decision have been better for the teachers or the students? Through collaborative professional dialogue, the class leader agreed that the students had been struggling with the text. We made the decision to be proactive and to work together to adapt the curriculum overview to incorporate a different text. We made a decision that was focused on the learning outcomes of the students. Students' learning must be at the centre of everything that we do and it's worthwhile for us to consider all the factors that potentially distract us from maintaining this focus.

Experiences of teacher learning in schools

I am arguing in this book that the more reflective and thoughtful that you are, and the more proactive you are in engaging in professional learning, the better the teacher that you will become. You will develop a greater self-confidence as a teacher, with a strong evidence-based knowledge of the most effective pedagogies and strategies to enable the best possible learning outcomes for your students. However, my research has also acknowledged that this process is not always a straightforward one for the teachers in our schools. This is because, despite the core business of our schools being 'learning', my research has reflected that the quality of teacher learning experiences in schools is often relatively poor. The quality of the learning environments for teachers still leaves significant room for improvement in most schools. By becoming thinking teachers, my expectation is for you to both improve your own teaching skills and positively influence the quality of the learning environment in which you work.

Ideally, the environment in your school should foster a collaborative learning culture. This can be achieved through the development of a culture of trust and mutual accountability, in which teachers plan together, research together, evaluate together and learn together. However, the pervading culture in many schools does not naturally foster collaborative learning and teachers are often reluctant to open up their practice and to share the concerns that they may have. A thinking teacher is brave in sharing their concerns about their practice including challenges that they may be facing. I can accept that this can be difficult within a leadership culture that is dominated by control, compliance and judgement. Robinson (2018) has discussed the underlying beliefs and concerns that prevent teachers from changing their behaviours, particularly in relation to trialling changes to their practice. She argues that teachers are often afraid to voice their concerns because they may be worried about opening up their practice for fear of being judged. In my own doctoral thesis, the most valued professional learning opportunity shared by all staff was the value of collaborative learning – this can be a challenge in many schools. Remember that we must remain focused on our own continual learning and growth but equally, we must also be determined in influencing the learning environment in which we work.

I would argue that colleagues of mine became curious about the strategies I was developing in my classroom during my NQT year, as a consequence of my master's degree studies. For example, during my first term as a teacher, I introduced a peer reading programme in my classroom. This involved the training of more fluent readers in the classroom as reading mentors, who were then paired up to support the reading development of less confident readers. There was a clearly structured approach to how I introduced this programme, to reflect the range of research studies that I had investigated. Through the use of action research as a methodology and the need to articulate my findings in a written assignment, there was also a structured approach to both the implementation and evaluation of the strategy. In the second term, the English coordinator at the school came to find out about what I was doing and was so impressed that he asked me to share my strategy with the rest of the staff team at a staff meeting after school. I feel that this particular event reflects the value of becoming a thinking teacher in the fact that I was not only actively reflecting upon and improving my own teaching practice but also influencing practice across the school. In the thinking school, every person, regardless of their years of service, is expected to be a thinking teacher. Imagine the quality of the collaborative learning environment if every member of staff is working in this way, and imagine the potential learning outcomes of the students who attend such a school.

I have been a headteacher of three different schools and my aim in each school has been to develop a collaborative learning community, in which all teachers are able to plan, research and learn together. Each time I have been faced with challenges. However, these challenges usually come from the leaders at the school or those that have been tasked to advise me, rather than the teachers. Those leaders or teachers that have been successful in traditionally hierarchical environments, dominated by direction and monitoring from above, can find it challenging when I move to a more distributed leadership model, with a greater focus on teacher autonomy. In my first ever term as headteacher, I inherited a staff team that had been informed by Ofsted that it 'requires improvement' six weeks earlier. I also inherited a teaching team that was very enthusiastic but were 'on their knees' due to a culture of over-monitoring and individual judgements. A team that had experienced insufficient opportunities for collaborative learning and were used to being 'told what to do' and never to question what they were being asked to do. They were afraid to open up their practice because they had become scarred by lesson observations that graded their teaching and provided insufficient direction for their learning and improvement.

I explained to my school improvement partner (SIP) at the time that my first intention as headteacher would be to enable all teachers to develop their understanding of the craft of teaching and learning and that we would do this through engaging in collaborative action research projects. We would move away from judgemental graded lesson observations and introduce a model of peer learning observations, characterised by reflective collaborative professional dialogue. I was informed by my SIP that the teachers and the learning community at the school were not ready for such an approach and that I personally needed to observe each teacher and provide them with a judgement of their teaching – a choice of 'inadequate', requiring improvement', 'good' or 'outstanding' (as if anyone is likely to be motivated by being told they are inadequate!) – and set targets for improvement. I was also warned that Ofsted would return within 18 months and that if the school was subsequently judged to not have improved sufficiently, I was in danger of losing my job.

Essentially, I was being told that the route to improve teaching in the classroom was to trust teachers less and direct and control more. I still believe this remains the pervading approach in many of our schools! I am certain that having read so far, you may consider this to be the opposite approach if you wish to develop thinking teachers. Well, despite the advice of my SIP, I stuck with my original plan, much to the delight of many teachers across the school. We made the decision to actively develop thinking teachers and a thinking school. We used the findings of those collaborative action research projects in that first term to inform our policy for teaching and learning at the school, written by the teachers. I am very proud to say that those teachers that were told that they were 'requiring improvement' were the same teachers that led our school to an Ofsted judgement of 'outstanding' a few years later. We did this by using the approaches I discuss in this book. Many of those teachers are now leading and developing teams of thinking teachers and will no doubt go on to lead thinking schools in the future.

I have always felt that outdated approaches to school improvement reflect the influence of government policy in the UK over the past 30 years in promoting teacher learning through short-term externally developed courses. In the example presented, the notion presented by external consultants was that action research would be 'more appropriate' for a school that was in a stronger position and more successful. I was told that it would be better to send teachers on one-day courses entitled, 'From Good to Outstanding'. I was informed by some teachers that they had been sent on courses with no explanation as to the rationale for doing so. I am not saying that these types of courses are not useful. However, my own research and experiences suggest that teacher learning activities such as these often provide 'sticking plasters' and may improve performance in the short term but do not encourage deeper reflection. There is often insufficient time for teachers to then reflect upon how any changes introduced have impacted directly upon students' learning. Teachers need to have both the tools and the time to develop the skills to undertake this type of reflection effectively, and I will discuss this later in the book. Too many schools and teachers remain dependent on outside intervention to direct their professional learning instead of exploiting the informal and formal learning opportunities available in every school. My experience demonstrates that many leaders in schools have not been able to develop the skills and knowledge to build the structures and cultures in schools to promote an expansive learning environment or to develop thinking teachers. However, I do believe that all teachers are capable of becoming thinking teachers and all schools becoming thinking schools.

Summary

In this first chapter, I have called for the need to reconceptualise our view on the role of the teacher and what constitutes effective teacher professional learning. A study of international reviews of effective teacher professional learning (Cordingley et al, 2015) has highlighted the significance of sustained learning activities over time that additionally facilitate experimentation in the classroom. The thinking teacher is one that is as equally concerned with their own learning as they are with their students' learning. I envisage each thinking teacher to be a potential Master of Education who is actively engaging in research, continually experimenting and trialling changes to their practice in order to improve their craft year on year. Consider the environment in which you are working and the extent to which you are able to do this. Take every opportunity you can to engage in professional learning. Do not become the teacher that learns to play safe or stops improving in their third year of teaching.

I have shared the importance of examining and defining your 'why' – of examining your motivations and underlying values and how these impact upon your teaching practice in the classroom. I have done this because the first step in becoming a thinking teacher is to consciously develop a mindset to do so. In my first year of teaching, I made the decision to attempt to become the best teacher that I could possibly be, and I realised that my professional learning would be central to my improvement. I have maintained that mindset and focus throughout my career. I believe that you need to have that mindset of restlessness and inquiry in an ongoing cycle of critical reflection and improvement. I have discussed the importance of engaging in key formal learning activities and how this will enable you to benefit from the energy of 'informal learning'. Take every opportunity to engage in collaborative professional learning with your colleagues and develop a mindset of learning-focused teaching.

Relevant reading

Atwal, K. (2019) *The Thinking School*. Woodbridge: John Catt.

Cordingley, P., Higgins, S., Greany, T., Buckler, N., Coles-Jordan, D., Crisp, B., Saunders, L. and Coe, R. (2015) Developing Great Teaching: Lessons from the international reviews into effective professional development. Teacher Development Trust.

Fuller, A., Hodkinson, H., Hodkinson, P. and Unwin, L. (2005) 'Learning as peripheral participation in communities of practice: a reassessment of key concepts in workplace learning', *British Education Research Journal* 31 (1) pp. 49-68.

Kanter, R. M. (1977) *Men and women of the corporation*. New York: Basic Books.

Kraft, M. A. and Papay, J. P. (2016) 'The Myth of the Performance Plateau', *Educational Leadership*, May, pp. 36-42.

Robinson, V. (2011) *Student-centered leadership.* San Francisco: Jossey-Bass.

Robinson, V. (2018) *Reduce Change to Increase Improvement.* Thousand Oaks, CA: Sage.

Reflective questions

1. What is your motivation for becoming a teacher?
2. What excites you most about teaching?
3. What kind of teacher would you like to become? How would you want your students to describe you?
4. How will you ensure that you maintain continual improvement as a teacher?
5. How would you describe the learning environments for teachers in the schools that you have worked in?
6. What do you think you can do to influence and improve the professional learning environment in your current school?

Chapter 2
Developing as a Thinking Teacher

The Thinking Classroom

Teaching is certainly a very complicated job and in my opinion a job that you will never completely master. Rather than seeing this as a daunting prospect, I view this to be one of the reasons that it is such an enjoyable and rewarding profession. I love the fact that I am in a profession in which I am continually learning, growing and developing. I enjoy the challenge of knowing that every student in every class I teach is unique, and that the experience of teaching each student is different. I may become expert in many aspects of my teaching practice but there will always be surprises and room for improvement. The complex nature of the profession and the day-to-day demands of teaching will ensure that there is always something to do. As a teacher, I knew that I could stay in my classroom until midnight and there would still be more to do. The purpose of this book is to enable you to effectively manage the challenges you will undoubtedly face; to not become overwhelmed by them and to embrace them. I urge you to become a thinking teacher to manage these challenges in a way in which you can maximise both your students' learning and your own, while enjoying the fantastic job that teaching can undoubtedly be.

The prerequisite for developing a thinking classroom is to ensure that you have the right conditions for learning in place in your classroom. Therefore, at the start of this second chapter, we are going to think briefly about the type of classroom you are going to nurture and develop. How will the students feel when they are in your classroom? What will they say? What will they value? What will they think? What will they do? In chapter 1, I asked you to consider your vision of a great teacher and a great school. Take time to consider the type of teacher you really want to be. I think the easiest way to do this is to consider what you want for your students, and the impact you want to have on them over the time you are teaching them and beyond.

Returning to the complexity of the profession, let's outline for a moment some of the challenges that we face as teachers. I've highlighted a few in the following list and this is certainly not exhaustive.

1. How do we ensure that every student is challenged in every lesson that we teach? That we are able to take into account prior learning and sufficiently motivate and challenge every child to build on their prior learning.

2. How do we manage the behaviour in the classroom so that every student is focused?

3. How do we manage that behaviour yet ensure that every student feels relaxed, safe, valued and has a voice?

4. How do we ensure that our teaching not only develops our students academically but also personally, socially and emotionally?

5. How do we organise the classroom in such a way that our students can work effectively in pairs, threes, groups, collectively and independently?

6. How do we ensure that our students are intrinsically and extrinsically motivated to learn?

7. How do we ensure effective curriculum coverage yet allow students to lead their learning too?

8. How do we ensure that our students respect and listen to the teacher as well as maintaining really positive learning relationships?

9. How do we ensure that all students have access to positive and developmental feedback?

10. How do we balance our time between whole class teaching and working with individuals or groups of students?

This list represents just a few potential challenges faced by teachers and I'm sure you can add several more. The reason I present this list at this point is not to overwhelm you. I would urge you to embrace this list and I would argue that if you become a thinking teacher and develop the right conditions for learning in your classroom, you can both embrace and effectively meet these various challenges. But you will need to begin by really thinking deeply about these conditions for learning and the type of classroom that you would like to lead.

We are going to begin this process with a thinking activity. I do not want you to think as a teacher however. More importantly, I want you to think as a learner. I want you to take the opportunity to think about a time in your life when you have had a really positive learning experience. It might be an experience from your school days or as an adult. Additionally, I would like you to think about a really negative learning experience. Take yourself back to those moments and consider how you were feeling on each of these occasions. Really try to picture how you felt and consider the physical and social conditions around you when you engaged in these learning activities. What factors helped you to learn and what factors hampered your learning? How did the teacher/trainer influence how you were feeling and the extent to which you were successful? What was easy about the learning experience and what was challenging? Most importantly I want you to really reflect upon how you felt before, during and after the experience. I would suggest that you close the book and take some time to really reflect upon these experiences.

Thinking time...

Why do you think I have asked you to undertake this learning experience?

Firstly, it is important to understand ourselves as learners if we are to become thinking teachers. Secondly, it is important to always consider the point of view of our students. How is our teaching making them feel, and how positive a learning experience is it for them to be in our classrooms. Whenever I'm working with a new group of teachers, I always ask them to undertake this thinking activity. In positive learning experiences, example responses will include the feeling of: being valued; listened to; the teacher genuinely cared, believed in them, gave them confidence; they were challenged yet felt safe; they were able to take risks and weren't afraid of making mistakes. In negative experiences, they were made to feel the opposite: that they would never get it; under pressure; even frightened. I then ask them to share their thoughts in groups and come up with 10 principles or ideas that they believe will support learning and how these can be adapted to their students' learning. This is always our starting point to develop the right conditions for learning in our classrooms to enable our students to thrive. As mentioned earlier, I don't believe that any interaction between a teacher and student is neutral in its impact – it is either positive or negative. As a thinking teacher, we have to create the right conditions for learning in our classroom to ensure that it is a positive learning environment for all students.

Each time I undertake this activity, the list that the participants come up with will differ slightly. However, they are always overwhelmingly positive. Take the time now to consider the type of learning environment you want to create. Don't worry too much about the detail. However, do think about how you want your students to feel in your classroom. Before I began teaching my first class, I was given a lot of advice by my colleagues. Like many beginner teachers, one of my greatest concerns was around behaviour, and I will talk about behaviour for learning specifically later in the book. Would the children behave for me? Will they listen to me? Will they respect me? One piece of advice I was given was to not 'smile until Christmas'! It certainly makes me smile looking back now because I didn't even make it to playtime on the first day! Despite my best efforts to be firm and not smile, one of the reasons I love my job is because children love to smile and teaching makes me smile. What I learned by playtime on my first day of teaching was the fact that the students were more worried about what I would be like than I was ever worried about them. As I will mention countless times, the most important thing for me is to build fantastic relationships with my students. This is the key to enabling their learning. Critics of this approach may argue instead for a zero tolerance approach and the need to be firm to really enable all students to behave and learn. Without going into too much detail at this point, that first school in which I taught was also a resourced provision school. I was teaching a number of children with profound and multiple learning needs as well as children with extreme emotional and behavioural needs within a mainstream setting. I was working with students who in many other local education authorities would have been placed and taught in specialist provision schools. I very quickly realised that one of my core values was to enable my students to feel listened to and valued. By doing so, I could be more effective in challenging each student to learn and achieve.

I have detailed examples on the following pages that one group of teachers came up with when undertaking this conditions for learning activity and ask you to consider the extent to which you think they relate to the conditions that you wish to create in your own classroom.

1. **Positive role model**. See yourself as the lead learner in the classroom. You are modelling the skills and attitudes to learning that you want your students to develop. For example, if you want your students to develop their critical thinking skills, model your own critical thinking. Consider also your hidden influence. The way in which you talk to your students and colleagues is implicitly modelling to them how you expect them to talk to each other and to their teachers.

2. **Calm learning environment**. How do we create a sense of calm in our classrooms? Often, as inexperienced teachers, we will look to the students and their behaviours in setting the emotional climate and relative calmness in the classroom. However, as is discussed throughout this book, it is really important for us to consider ourselves in terms of our values and actions, and how these influence the emotional climate in the classroom. We are the mood makers in the classroom and our behaviours will influence the learning environment. We can consider this both in terms of structures and cultures and I will discuss these further later in the book. Children are very intuitive and will internalise

the expectations that adults hold of them in the classroom. In secondary schools in particular, most students are very adept at adapting behaviour, according to the expectations and emotional climate of each individual classroom they enter.

When speaking to a group of secondary aged students recently, their comments reflected exactly the point made. They were very aware of what was expected in each classroom. They wanted teachers to control the class but, equally, they wanted teachers to listen to them and allow them to be themselves, building good relationships with them. They are very aware of the expectations in terms of structures and cultures. In terms of structures, I'm talking about the rules and routines you promote in the classroom. Clear routines, promoted consistently, are crucial in providing structure for your students, and this structure will provide a sense of emotional security. Consistency is key and supports the development of a culture that promotes emotional security. If, as a learner, I know that I will have the opportunity to speak and share my thinking, or my misconceptions, this will give me a sense of safety.

Reflection begins with conversations with ourselves so take time to consider how you will promote a calm learning environment. This self-reflection is crucial. In my first year I noticed that when my students were getting louder, my voice would tend to get louder. I reflected on this and implemented a new strategy. Whenever I felt my voice getting louder, I would self-adjust and bring the volume of my voice down. This would initiate a sense of calmness. I would also always ensure that I never spoke over someone else. We are the models remember and the way in which we conduct ourselves in the classroom, within a culture of mutual respect, is modelling to our students how we expect them to conduct themselves too.

3. **Enthusiasm and passion.** Remember that these are the conditions that a single group of teachers decided upon! Sometimes I will hear people ask why they would need to be 'passionate' as teachers. That it is the responsibility of students to learn, regardless of the particular approach undertaken by the teacher. The reason I am writing about becoming a thinking teacher is because, as a professional, I want to get the very best out of myself. As a leader, I want to get the very best

out of those I lead. As teachers, I believe it is important that we are both enthusiastic and passionate about the subject(s) that we teach as well as the students that we are teaching. If I am not enthusiastic about the subject matter I am presenting, how can I expect my students to be enthusiastic and motivated to learn in that subject? Equally, if I'm not authentically passionate about ensuring that every student in my class succeeds, it is likely that not every student will. Remember that I repeatedly say that the student will internalise the expectations that teachers hold of them. It is my responsibility to be enthusiastic about my students' learning and development. I accept that I need to have strong subject knowledge. Equally, I need to develop a strong understanding of each individual student that I am teaching and exactly where they are in their learning. That does not mean treating every student equally. It means developing an equitable classroom in which each student is given the individual personalised learning support that they need.

4. **Mutual respect**. As the lead learner and model in the classroom, it is crucial that I am promoting a culture of mutual respect. Not every teacher is going to agree with my perspective in this book and that is fine. If teaching was a straightforward job, with simple transferable strategies, I would be writing a teaching manual. It is complex and therefore it is important that we adhere to some straightforward principles to enable us to adapt to this inherent complexity. That is why I believe it is so important to create a culture of mutual respect in the classroom. I am modelling my expectations for behaviour to the students I teach. I believe that if I am not treating each and every child I teach, or colleagues I work alongside, with respect, then I cannot expect my students and colleagues to do the same with each other.

Every school I have led has become a UNICEF Rights Respecting school. At the centre of everything that we do is the recognition that all children are entitled to the rights enshrined within the United Nations Convention on the Rights of the Child. These rights are unalienable and apply to every child, and article 28 is the right to an education. I wish to teach and lead in a way that is underpinned by an unflinching respect for those I teach and those

I lead. Mutual respect is important because it underpins the values we hold in our classroom and our schools. It sets the culture in the school to enable all within the classroom or learning community to be themselves and express themselves, with the expectation that this is done with respect.

5. **Respect and value all contributions and efforts**. This condition may seem similar to the previous one or even straightforward and easily dismissed. However, in an authentic thinking classroom, I believe it is essential to consider the level of equity. In reflecting upon our classroom environment, it is useful to consider the extent to which we authentically value all contributions and efforts in the classroom. What opportunities do we take to do this and are we actively aware of the times we do this and how this consequently makes our students feel? We want to create a culture in our classrooms in which our students learn to associate effort with success, rather than ability. An attitude which demonstrates to them that the harder they work on the task the more likely they are to succeed. That is why it is really important that we take opportunities to value the contributions and efforts that our students make and articulate clearly to them how those efforts lead to their progress in their learning and success.

For example, how often do we stop at the right answer?! I will give an example of what I mean by this. The dominant discourse of engagement in typical classrooms is: teacher asks a question. Student responds. Teacher responds. If the response of the student is incorrect, we will then ask if anybody else has a response to share: student responds. Teacher responds. And we continue this way until we arrive at the right answer. We may then respond with 'well done' or 'excellent'. And for those who hadn't arrived at the right answer, we might attempt to make them feel better by saying, 'good try' or 'nearly'.

Now let's take the time to review this exchange and consider how we could use the discussion as a more meaningful learning activity and engage a wider range of students in the classroom. How about if we asked the same question and took the same response from the student. Do we sometimes say 'good try' or 'nearly' to students even when they aren't close or it isn't really a good try? Respecting your students means also providing authentic responses. Consider for a moment what you want to achieve with your students. I would always say that I want my students to be self-reflective, independent, critical thinkers. Consequently, I would aim to ensure that my students are engaged in deeper reflection and thinking for longer periods in the classroom. Returning to the original scenario, instead of responding, don't say anything at all. Leave a space and see what happens.

We are going to do this because most classroom activities encourage the development of an environment in which students become accustomed to looking for the answer that is in the teacher's head. In the thinking classroom, the thinking teacher is as equally interested in the answers that are in the students' heads. Again, this doesn't preclude the value of direct instruction. Instead, it encourages the development of dialogue in the classroom and chains of inquiry. You do not respond at all to the first response and instead will write the answer on the board/flipchart. You then write the next student's response without having committed to giving any verbal feedback. You write every answer you receive on the board, close or not, right or wrong, and you are demonstrating to every child that you value and respect every answer. This encourages both deeper thinking and the opportunity for self-correction. As the students reflect upon all these recorded answers, they take opportunities to think more deeply. Some students will then decide to change their answers, having reflected more deeply. Can you see that this exchange provides a more deeper and open learning exchange than the original example? Rather than giving your opinions and responding to every answer you receive, you could ask the students to say if they agree or disagree. By extending this exchange, not only are the children encouraged to think more deeply but equally, the teacher gains a deeper understanding of the thinking and current learning/knowledge of a wider range of students.

Matthew Syed, in his book *Rebel Ideas* (2019), provides us with a similar example to this when discussing the leadership of staff meetings. He argues that junior members within a team may fail to speak up because of fear of the perceived leader of the team. In our case in the thinking classroom, the leader is the teacher, and the students are the junior members. Remember, the thinking classroom is dependent upon an environment in which every child has the confidence in which to share their thinking. Syed argues that leaders are positioned as not only powerful but also smart. It is not difficult to transfer these power dynamics to those typically seen in classrooms. The locus of control and power sits with the teacher. Equally, the locus of knowledge also sits with a teacher. After all, isn't that the role of the teacher, to impart and share their knowledge and mastery of the subject with the students?

Syed goes on to argue that most important decisions are taken within the many millions of meetings that take place across the world every day. He explains that most meetings are inefficient and dysfunctional, particularly in terms of communication. Many people are silent and status rigs the discourse. People don't say what they think but what they think the leader wants to hear. If we transfer these findings to my experiences in the classroom, too often students are either silent and potentially disengaged, or unwilling to share their own thoughts for fear of getting things wrong. Would this continue to be the case if we were to begin to value 'wrong' answers as much as we value the 'right' answer? Would this raise the number of contributions made by children, and the level of engagement in thinking and dialogue? You may think that there isn't a problem with aiming to find the right answer or look for the answer that is in the teacher's head. After all, surely the teacher is the expert and it is their job to share their knowledge. I do not disagree with the value of this in some aspects of learning. However, it can also present limitations in developing inquiry, critical thinking and reasoning skills. This is why it is important to not always respond, to value every answer, and to give your students the time and space to both engage in and articulate their own thinking. By giving thinking time to children and using mini whiteboards for example, every student is presenting their own unique response and answer. Rather than an answer that has been influenced and interpreted through the response of another student, or by being unduly worried about the right answer in the teacher's head. We do this by valuing all responses.

I have had the privilege of visiting the lovely city of Oslo to support schools there in developing 'thinking classrooms'. I was asked to present my philosophy to a group of school leaders at a conference. I explained that I didn't feel comfortable in doing this until I had actually visited some schools in Oslo. I didn't want to just share my experiences of working in schools in England and I wanted to develop a better contextual understanding of the experiences of students in Oslo schools. On one such visit, I had the opportunity to participate in a grade 10 maths lesson. During this visit, I sat at the only spare seat in the classroom, alongside a young girl called Andrea. Despite the lesson being taught in Norwegian, I could see that the teacher was enabling the children to understand how to calculate the circumference and area of a circle. The teacher was clearly working incredibly hard during this lesson. (I always say that in a thinking classroom, the students should be thinking and working much harder than the teacher.) Yet, of the 20+ students in the class, only about five contributed and only those students that raised their hands were invited to speak. The teacher asked a question, took a response as soon as the hand went up, and stopped as soon as she arrived at the right answer. There was no thinking time and no questioning of the vast majority of children, who appeared passive in their learning engagement.

At the end of the lesson, I had the opportunity to ask Andrea a few questions. I asked her why she didn't put her hand up. A: 'I never put my hand up in class'. Me: 'Why not? A: 'I'm worried about getting it wrong.' Me: 'Why?' A: 'If I get it wrong or say I don't understand, then the other children may laugh at me. And the teacher will think I wasn't listening.' I am presenting this example because the learning opportunities for Andrea were not being maximised in this learning environment. Opportunities to enable Andrea to engage in deeper thinking and reflection were being missed. To an observer she would appear well-behaved and compliant, and appeared to be listening. More importantly, how much had she actually learned during the lesson? Like many students in similar learning environments around the world, Andrea attributed her lack of understanding to her own ability in maths rather than on anything to do with the work of the teachers. I would describe this type of student as 'educationally truant'. Although she was attending school, her learning engagement was not being maximised. As a thinking teacher, I want and require my students to be more demanding of me. If they don't understand fully what I'm trying to explain to them or have misconceptions, I absolutely need to know that. Otherwise we are missing really valuable learning opportunities for all. By respecting and valuing all contributions and efforts, we move towards a more equitable environment in which listening to each other, including misconceptions, is as important a learning opportunity as listening to the teacher.

6. **Awareness of external factors.**

   I always talk about the need to take every opportunity possible to get to know your students. What is going on in their minds, how are they feeling, what factors may be affecting the extent to which they are able to access and engage in the learning opportunities on offer? As a school leader, I believe it is my responsibility to consider the learning needs of the staff I lead in exactly the same way that I want them to consider the learning needs of their students. This includes a consideration of the social and emotional factors that may be affecting their capacity to teach. As teachers, we are not robots. There may be times in our teaching careers where external factors in our lives may be impacting on us. It is important that our school is a learning environment in which staff feel confident that it is a safe place to share their concerns. By doing this, we then encourage our teachers to do the same for their students.

   Equally, your students are not robots. They are all complex and unique personalities and their readiness to learn will be affected by their personal, social and emotional wellbeing. Take the time to become aware, where appropriate, of external factors that may potentially affect your students' wellbeing and learning. Consider your classroom environment and the extent to which it is one that children feel safe to share their inner emotions in. I always encourage our teachers to take opportunities to find out wider information about their students. Do they have siblings? Do they have to share a bedroom? Where do they do their homework? Do they walk to school? Do they have a morning routine? Do they eat breakfast? You may consider some of these questions to be intrusive but they will give you insight into the wider life experiences of your students and this may well support you in decisions that you make in your planning and teaching. Equally, they will demonstrate to your students that you are not just their teacher in the classroom, that you care about their wider education and development. Learning does not begin and end within the school day, it continues throughout your students' lives and it is important to value and acknowledge this.

When I was on my PGCE, I was advised by a guest lecturer that we should take every opportunity available to understand the life experiences of the people within our school community. I now consider this to be what I describe as 'servant leadership'. One way of defining servant leadership is through a focus on serving the needs of our children and families. To do this we build a learning community built upon collaboration and high trust. As a headteacher, it is important for me to understand the needs of those I lead. So, we are creating a learning community in which we are consciously aware of taking every opportunity to understand our students and the community that they come from. An example a guest lecturer gave us was to park your car further away from your school or get off the bus or train one-stop earlier. I was fascinated by this. She was arguing that by walking the streets of your community, you gain a deeper understanding of the life experiences of your students. Throughout that particular placement, I spent some time in the warren of streets that surrounded this particular primary school in which I was placed. I got to know the people in the community, and this helped me build positive relationships with the students and families that I was serving, many of whom were living in very challenging circumstances. I realised that I wouldn't have been able to do this if I drove in and out of the school car park each day. Many of the parents had had negative experiences of schooling when they had been children themselves and school could have been seen as an intimidating setting. I actively worked to break down some of those barriers. In every school that I've worked, I've made every effort possible to walk to school and get to know and understand the local community. Many years later that was the reason I was determined to spend time in the streets of Oslo and within the schools before undertaking any presentation for school leaders there.

7. **Different types of learning activities.**

I really enjoy teaching. I enjoy it because every individual lesson and every day is different and every student that I teach is unique. This, of course, provides great challenge to any teacher, but also creative opportunities too. Take time when planning to consider the different types of activities that you wish your students to engage in to support their learning. Remember that the key is to inspire and motivate each student to actively engage. If your students are self-motivated and actively engaged in the subject matter, teaching can be more of a straightforward experience. It's not about putting on a 'show' for the children, it is about considering the range of learning activities you can offer and also the variety of experiences.

For example, there will be times when you engage in 'direct instruction'. Where you may be modelling a strategy and all the students are required to listen in silence. Equally, this example of direct instruction will be followed by opportunities for children to practice, rehearse and sharpen their knowledge and skills. This may be done within a range of independent learning, paired work, learning trios, or larger group work. There may be whole-class discussion where you use a range of open and closed questions. You may ask questions of all the children or direct, differentiated questioning for individuals. Consider also the range of resources you deploy. Your students may be demonstrating their learning through writing, speaking, drawing or even acting. What technology will you deploy to engage the children? When learning about volcanoes, for example, you could show video clips of erupting volcanoes or even build your own volcano. The key is to consider the range of learning activities you have at your disposal to engage and motivate all your students.

8. **Encourage and praise to build confidence.**

During my career in education, I must have visited and seen over a thousand different classrooms and lessons. I can tell you that there has not been one lesson in all that time where I felt there had been too much praise. In fact I would argue the opposite. As long as the praise is evaluative and authentic, as discussed earlier, you should take every opportunity possible to praise your students and you should see this to be a central part of your role. Do not assume that your students automatically know what it is that they are doing well and what factors are leading to their success as learners. When working with teachers, I describe the process as one of appreciative enquiry – a process where we actively articulate the strengths of those we lead. If I'm watching a lesson, it is the process through which I enable the teacher to understand the actions, values, strategies and activities the teacher is articulating/ deploying in order for them to understand what it is they are doing that is successful. This is as important as identifying areas for improvement. It will enable teachers to understand how they can continue to replicate these strategies again in the future for repeated success. This will also build confidence in a teacher's own awareness and understanding of the job. I will share a model for teachers to use to engage in your own process of appreciative enquiry in chapter 4. As a teacher, it is equally important to have a conscious understanding of what you are doing that is working well and is successful, as it is to identify your areas for improvement.

If we translate this to the student level, the key is to ensure that students are aware of what they are doing well in order to build on that success. This is relevant to the development of knowledge as well as skills. I always take opportunities to articulate clearly the skills that the children have deployed that has been successful. This may be related to the efforts they have made, the questions they have asked, the misconceptions they have addressed, or even the mistakes and challenges they have overcome. This is designed to directly build their confidence in themselves as learners. They begin to understand the factors that have led to their success in this particular situation and this builds confidence in themselves in similar challenging learning situations; they have the experience of persevering and succeeding that they can draw upon. Our job is to build learning capacity and evaluative praise is a crucial tool in enabling us to do that. Praise can also be addictive. The more we receive it, the more likely we will work towards seeking it out again in the future. In a student teacher relationship, this is even more likely to happen and even more powerful if the praise is received from someone whose opinion we authentically believe, value and respect. This evaluative praise will enable you to build upon your students' metacognitive strategies and I will discuss this further in chapter 5.

9. **High expectations.**

I read recently in a magazine that some educators held concerns about the value of holding high expectations. The argument is that it can place unnecessary pressure on children, encouraging them to judge themselves negatively if they fail to meet the high expectations of the teachers. I hope you agree that, having read this far into the book, the thinking teacher in the thinking classroom deliberately designs opportunities for children to become empowered and confident learners. The purpose of having high expectations is not to unduly place pressure on students but actually to take pressure off. To enable them to understand that they don't need to view learning as one-off lessons but as a process that happens and develops over time. Having high expectations is also about knowing that learning isn't a linear process and that we will face challenges over time. High expectations is about comparing ourselves to our previous best, not to the student next to us, and knowing that if we put the necessary effort in, we will continue to improve.

I believe that having high expectations for our students is about not placing unnecessary limitations and caps on our students' learning. My experience of our education system has reflected a focus on differentiating tasks for children by ability groups. We are even happy to use the terms higher ability, middle ability, lower ability. By giving these groups different tasks, are we placing limitations on what the students are able to achieve in that lesson? Remember that students are likely to internalise the expectations held by their teachers. If I am placed in the third set for science in year 10, is there consequently a ceiling on what I can potentially achieve at GCSE? Will I internalise and believe that, despite my best efforts, I couldn't possibly secure as good a grade as those in set one?

I advocate high expectations most prominently because I see the damage caused by low expectations. The thinking teacher will really take the time to reflect upon their own unconscious biases. To what extent may we hold lower expectations of some students based upon their gender, race, learning needs, language, social status? A subtle difference to the activities detailed is to ensure all children can attempt all the differentiated activities if they choose to. Say to students that they are doing the first activity because it reflects their current understanding in the subject. Additionally, enable them to believe that once they have successfully completed it, they will be able to move onto the next activity that is more challenging. Remember we want all students to believe that through effort, they can succeed. If you are reading this and thinking, well some students will never get there, what does that say about the potential expectations that you may hold?

In every alternative workplace that I have had the opportunity to visit during my doctoral research, the overriding belief was that they needed to continually improve or they could be surpassed by their competitors. Learning organisations are continually striving to improve. In the hairdressing salon I visited, they are not using the same materials and resources for cutting hair in exactly the same way as they were ten years ago. They are aware that they have to grow and innovate to be successful. Do we do this enough in schools? Shouldn't schools be continually improving in such a way that, every year, students will improve on the achievements of the previous cohort in a continual cycle of improvement? If you don't believe this, why not, and what does it say about your expectations? A thinking teacher is continually looking to learn and improve. As discussed earlier, in an average year six class in my current school, more than 20 children can write as well as maybe four or five could in the first class that that I ever taught. If you had told me that 20 years ago, I probably wouldn't have believed you. Maybe this was because my expectations of my students weren't high enough. When I took on my first headship, the outcomes in the previous year saw only 60% of the children leave the school aged eleven with the expected levels of literacy and numeracy in the previous year. Within a few years, 90% of the children in year six at the school were surpassing those expectations. Many of these children were siblings of the previous cohort. I am absolutely certain that one of the most important factors was that as headteacher, I completely transformed the expectations the teachers held for student outcomes at the school. By continually and authentically modelling and articulating those expectations, those that I led began to alter their expectations too.

10. **Positive and trusting relationships.**

Many people may disagree but central to my conception of the thinking teacher is the need to build really positive learning relationships with your students. I will take this further and share that in a thinking school, this extends to the collaborative learning relationships we also build with our colleagues. Teaching is a challenging and complex job but the most complex thing we are ever faced with is our students' brains. To really understand our students' brains and their thinking, it is imperative that we really build positive relationships. Firstly, if our students value, respect and trust us, they are more likely to be emotionally ready to learn. When we discuss the appropriate conditions for learning, remember your own learning experiences and what enabled you to feel confident and comfortable in your own learning. If your students have a positive relationship with you, they will be more comfortable in challenging themselves in your classroom. I started this section by mentioning people who disagree about the value of relationships. I would caveat that slightly by emphasising how 'trusting' relationships in a classroom between a student and teacher includes the importance of having clear and consistent structures and boundaries in place in terms of expectations for behaviour. This is important in maintaining the sense of emotional security for our students. However, the relationship is balanced less towards power and more towards mutual respect.

Secondly, we want to develop positive and trusting relationships because we want our children to feel safe to share their ideas, thoughts and misconceptions. I can honestly say that in many of my classroom experiences as a child, both at primary and secondary level, I did not feel emotionally safe and I did not trust that the teacher in front of me really believed in me or wanted the best for me. At times, I felt invisible. I respected the opinions of my friends more than the teacher. This caused me to misbehave and not focus on my learning. I was more interested in impressing my friends with my antics rather than focusing on the learning. I certainly didn't feel confident in sharing my misconceptions with my teachers. For a thinking teacher to be successful, you really need to consider and understand what your students are thinking, particularly in terms of their misconceptions. I have never taught two children who are completely the same as learners, every student is unique. Positive relationships, built upon mutual respect and trust, will give you the best opportunity to really get inside your students' minds.

Transformative teaching

Remember that becoming a thinking teacher is essentially about establishing your mindset first. Then it is about considering the practices that will support you to continually think, grow and reflect. These first two chapters are designed to enable you to establish your mindset, enabling you to visualise both the type of teacher that you want to be and the type of classroom you want to create for your students. In this section, I want you to consider the extent to which you can authentically be transformative in your teaching. We've talked about the power of high expectations and no limitations, and this relates both to our students and to ourselves as teachers. Being a transformative teacher is central in the thinking classroom. Transformative teaching is about both recognising the powerful positive transformative effect we can have on our students' learning and lives, and also about how you can continually transform your way of thinking and being in the classroom to improve your practice.

Often, I hear people being described as 'natural teachers'. I think this can be a distraction because it detracts from the varied and complex skillset that is required for one to be an excellent teacher. As long as we have the right motivators, attitudes and dispositions, we can all become great teachers. You just have to believe that by showing the necessary determination and commitment and by engaging in the professional learning activities described in this book, you will continue to improve as a teacher. Essentially, you have to believe in your own transformation to become an excellent teacher. You have to become a thinking teacher.

As a thinking teacher, you will believe and be aware that you are making a positive difference to your students, and I view this from a moral perspective. You have a moral responsibility to do everything within your own power to do the very best you can in terms of the education of your students. And this 'very best' must begin with a career long commitment to your own professional learning. When you become a teacher and work in a school, it is very easy to replicate what you see around you, without question. You see the habits, behaviours and actions of the experienced teachers around you and you may be inspired to replicate their excellent practices. There is nothing wrong with this and you will develop many skills through collaboration, observation and learning from others. However, replicating alone will not be transformative. To be transformative, you need to continually think, reflect and improve. I would urge you to continually and critically question the established practices in your schools, including your own. Transformation is not simply about changing, it is also about reimagining what is possible.

In my NQT year, I made a declaration that I would aim to become the best teacher in the world. I didn't do this because I genuinely believed that I would become the best teacher but because I wanted to set no limitations for myself. I was also excited about the fact that it was impossible for me to imagine what this 'great teacher' would look like. What I meant by this is that it couldn't be defined and so I could spend my entire career learning, growing and developing. I didn't want to play safe or just be as good as the best other teacher in my school. When I became a headteacher, I aspired to create a community of empowered learners who are continually engaged in transforming the school. I did not necessarily know what this would look like or what the impact would be at the time. I didn't want to visualise it too much because this could lead me to unnecessarily imposing low expectations or limitations on what we could achieve as a staff team.

This is a section that I hadn't planned to write but I have certainly enjoyed writing. Through being transformative, I will gladly accept that there are things I'm doing right now as a teacher, even after 20 years, or as a leader, that can and will be improved. That should not be seen as a daunting prospect, and instead, should be acknowledged and embraced. Tracy Goss (2016), in her leadership book *The Last Word on Power*, urges us to transform our relationship with risk-taking. Rather than seeing risks as threatening, we should consider it essential to our learning and growth. By taking risks and trialling changes to our practice, we will continue to learn and improve and that is the ultimate aim of the thinking teacher. I have often found that many teachers find change difficult, because it implies a negative association with their previous practice. I urge you to embrace transformational change as part of your responsibility as a teacher and central to your practice. For a thinking teacher, what is possible for you as a teacher in the future should not be determined by what has previously been possible for you or any of the excellent teachers in your school in the past. It is crucial for us to never set limitations for what we can achieve as individual teachers or schools or even education systems.

Summary

In this second chapter, I have invited you to consider the learning conditions that are important for you to develop and your expectations for the learning environment you will actively choose to cultivate and nurture in your classrooms. I invited you to undertake a thinking activity in which you reflected upon your own learning experiences, both positive and negative. How did you think, feel, succeed, fail during these learning activities and how can you use these learning experiences to inform your own teaching? Additionally, I urged you to consider the ways in which we can be brave and transformative in our teaching. In the next chapter, we will take this learning further and develop a deeper understanding of reflective practice and how this will support our continual learning and growth as thinking teachers.

Relevant reading

Goss, T. (2016) *The Last Word on Power*. New York: Doubleday.

Syed, M. (2019) *Rebel Ideas: The Power of Diverse Thinking*. London: John Murray.

Reflective questions

1. Take the time to define the type of classroom learning environment that you wish to develop.
2. How do you want your students to think, feel and learn in your classroom?
3. What conditions for learning will you seek to nurture in your classroom?
4. What conditions for learning do you feel you need to prioritise?
5. To what extent do you feel that you can be truly transformative in your classroom? What are the barriers?

Chapter 3

Developing reflective practice

When I was training to be a teacher, the buzz phrase at the time was reflective teaching. I would argue that reflective practice is at the core of what it means to be a thinking teacher. In this section, I will discuss why it is so important to be reflective and how we can engage in reflective practice strategies to enable us to develop the skills of reflection. The aim is for these skills to become central to our practice and way of working. The key thing to remember is that reflection always begins with conversations with ourselves. Regardless of the level of teaching experience we may have, we can always ask reflective questions of ourselves in an ongoing cycle of improvement. We do this to establish what we are doing well as teachers, as well as considering areas of our practice that we need to improve.

Let's take the time now to engage in a straightforward reflective activity; this is one I ask ECTs and student teachers to engage in when I am working with them. You can do this regardless of how experienced you are. Write down one thing that is going really well in your classroom, something that you believe you're really good at. Then write down one thing that you believe is not going so well, something that you really feel you need to improve and develop. Take the time to really think deeply about your teaching practice. Now consider why you think it is useful to engage in this type of reflection. The premise of this book is based on the assertion that teaching is an extremely complex job. It requires thinking teachers because throughout the working day, teachers are continually required to exercise their professional judgement. By reflecting on your practice, you begin to understand the underlying research and rationale for the professional judgements and decisions you make. By engaging in reflective practice and becoming a thinking teacher, the aim is for you to continue to develop your professional expertise. In this section I will share specific activities that you can engage in in order to develop your understanding of reflective practice and become a thinking teacher.

As discussed earlier in the book, there is research to show that the pace of teacher improvement begins to slow as we become more experienced. This may initially appear to be a natural progression as we move from novice to expert. However, it may also be because we become less reflective as we become more experienced. I find that ECTs are much more comfortable in discussing their areas for development than more experienced teachers because we don't always nurture learning climates in schools in which teachers feel safe to open up their practice and share their perceived 'weaknesses'. In the thinking school, all teachers are encouraged to collaborate and open up their practice. It should be seen as a strength to share your areas for improvement, rather than a sign of weakness. However, to encourage the development of such an environment we need to move away from a culture dominated by performance and judgement towards one of reflection and learning.

The term reflective teaching was first developed by John Dewey in 1933. He made the distinction between reflective action and routine action. Whereas routine is guided by the habit and typical expectations imposed through hierarchy or authority, reflection is about actively engaging in an examination of your practice. Whereas routine is static, reflection is about responding proactively to changing situations and circumstances. I feel that it is very easy for teachers to become stuck in 'routine action', holding onto strategies and techniques that may have served them well in the past. The key is to be able to move from the routine to the reflective, and that is why it is so important to develop the skills of reflective practice as early as possible in your career. I've maintained throughout this book that teaching is complex and, as a profession, one that we never completely master. Dewey believed that reflection was a tool to be used to make sense of events that are puzzling and is, therefore, perfect for teachers; a tool to enable us to make sense of the complexity in a cycle of continual improvement.

How would I define reflective practice? I would do it as simply as possible. Reflective practice is the ability to reflect on your own actions and the impact of those actions on the students that you teach. It is a process of self-evaluation to enable you to make changes to your practice in a process of continual learning and development. As a student teacher, I clearly saw the value of my engagement in reflective teaching. I saw the impact upon my teaching of daily engagement in reflection through cycles of reflective learning. Immediately after each lesson I taught, I completed a written evaluation. I remember that this was something my designated mentor at the time discouraged. He told me that I needed to go to the staffroom to engage with the other teachers and actually put this down as a target for my improvement. I chose to ignore his advice. I didn't want to lose these precious opportunities immediately after each lesson to engage in reflection. I was able to take the time to identify what had gone well as well as what I would like to do differently, in preparation for my next teaching opportunity. That is why I panicked at the start of my NQT year. I felt that I needed to continue to be supported, for example through engagement in research and relevant reading, in order to continue to reflect and improve.

In the following two figures, I have detailed two examples of researchers who have attempted to conceptualise the reflective learning cycle. Consider them in terms of your own practice. I believe that reflective practice is beautiful in its simplicity and the ease with which you can develop it as part of your teaching.

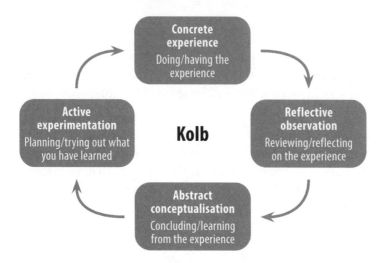

Figure 1: Kolb's learning cycle (1984)

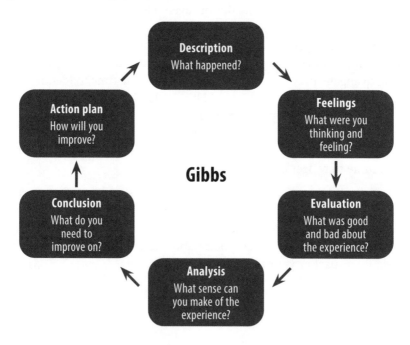

Figure 2: Gibbs' reflective cycle (1988)

Kolb and Fry (1975) considered the practice of reflection and created the learning cycle framework detailed in figure 1. Graham Gibbs (1988) further adapted the model (figure 2) to provide a framework of six stages through which a practitioner could examine and learn from repeated experiences. They are both cyclical models that allow you to learn from the things that have gone well as well as the things that haven't gone so well. There is a greater emphasis in this model on what you may have been thinking and feeling. So what does it look like in practice? The concrete experience takes place in terms of your day-to-day teaching practice. You are teaching a range of lessons every day of your working life. Unless you engage in reflection, the lessons can pass by in an experiential blur. You go from day to day without undertaking any conscious interpretation of the impact of your decision-making on the learning of your students. The first step, therefore, is to take the time to review and reflect upon your teaching. As discussed earlier, these reflections can begin with conversations with ourselves. However, under the right conditions, this reflection can be done collaboratively within a culture of high trust. The next step is to engage in new learning from these reflections. By considering what you have learned from your reflections, you then enter the zone of active experimentation. As a consequence of what you have learned from your reflections, you consider what you would like to do differently or what changes you wish to trial in your practice. You then make these changes as part of your concrete experiences and so begins the cycle again.

The reflective cycle model presented by Gibbs (1988) encourages you to reflect deeply on the lesson taught and consider what you were thinking and feeling at the time and to determine what worked/didn't work and why. The aim of the reflection is to make sense of and gain a deeper understanding of what happened. You can then identify an aspect of your practice that you may want to change and the experience begins again. For each of the stages you are required to reflect deeply and there are useful questions for you to consider.

Description
At this stage you are simply asked to describe the situation in detail, and you avoid discussing your thoughts, interpretations and feelings. You are

65

not expected to draw any conclusions as this will come at a later stage: what happened and how? Who was present? What did you do? What did your students do? What did you want to see happen? What were the outcomes?

Feelings

At this stage you consider your thoughts and feelings about the lesson/ interaction and how they may have impacted upon the outcomes: what were you feeling before, during, after the lesson? How did your students feel during the lesson and what might they be thinking and feeling now (you can extend these questions to include the thoughts and feelings of any other adults that may have been present)? What are you thinking about the lesson now?

Evaluation

The first two stages are designed to prepare you for the evaluation stage where you take the time to consider what went well and what didn't work during the lesson. Be as honest as you possibly can about the lesson, and it is really important to open up your practice. Remember that it is as equally important for you to evaluate what worked as well as what didn't work: what went well? What didn't go to plan? What positive contributions did you make? What negative contributions did you make?

Analysis

The analysis stage is designed for you to consider more deeply about why things worked or didn't work well. Up until now you have been concentrating on describing the details of the experience and now you are beginning to make sense of what happened during the lesson. This is, therefore, a very important stage in which you are analysing the different aspects of the lesson and considering why certain things went well while others didn't. You may want to draw upon areas of research or readings that you have undertaken to support your analysis. As thinking teachers, we are committed to engagement in research-based practice and this will support your engagement in reflective cycles: why did certain elements of the lesson go well? What enabled them to be successful? Why did certain elements not go so well? What have I learned about the different aspects of the lesson? What can help me make sense of the lesson (you may want to draw upon the support of colleagues or academic literature to support your analysis)?

Conclusions

At this stage you get the opportunity to make judgements about what happened during the lesson. This is where you take the opportunity to consider all that you have learned from the experience and decide upon the actions that you are going to commit to in order to further improve your teaching in the next lesson:

What have I learned about my teaching from this lesson? What have I learned about my students? How could I have improved my teaching in this lesson? What could I have done differently? What skills do I need to develop for me to improve my teaching? Who/what can support me in this improvement?

Action plan

At this stage you decide upon what you would like to do differently in future lessons and ways in which you are going to commit to change and improve your practice. You will need to consider how you are going to do this and who will support you. It is good practice to write these actions down in a reflective journal to support your learning: if I had to teach the same lesson again, what would I do differently? What am I going to do to help me develop the knowledge or skills I need to make these improvements to my practice? How will I ensure that I fully commit to making these changes to my practice?

I will repeat throughout this book that all the strategies that I advocate are complementary and interrelated. Reflective practice is a form of self-coaching and is designed to enable you to reflect deeply upon your practice within a continual cycle of improvement. It enables you to think as a teacher and will support you in developing thinking students too.

Examples of reflective practice

Remember that you don't need to be in a thinking school to become a thinking teacher. I'm writing this book to enable you to develop the requisite skills and become the best teacher you can possibly be for your students. However, your progress will be even more smooth and rapid if you are working in an environment where reflective practice is encouraged. The following points include examples of the activities that teachers in the schools I lead are routinely expected to engage in. These activities are designed to provide opportunities for teachers to reflect, think, learn and improve.

1. Ongoing reflection upon practice in the classroom

A teacher in England is expected to work 1265 hours per year, although we know that all teachers will work considerably more hours than that! My question for you here is to consider how well these hours are used to support teachers' professional learning. The official allocation of time designated to teachers' professional development is five teacher training days per year. To these five days we can add an hour or two per week designated for staff professional learning meetings after school. Consequently, the vast majority of time that teachers spend in school is in isolation in their classrooms, teaching lessons. By developing as a thinking teacher, you actively use this teaching time to engage in reflective practice as part of your ongoing professional learning. You will actively take opportunities, both during your teaching and immediately after your teaching, to reflect upon the impact of your teaching on your students. This will enable you to consider the outcomes of your practice and inform your future decision-making.

The examples of reflective practice cycles presented earlier describe a model in which reflective practice takes place through a series of stages. My argument for the need for teachers to engage in reflective practice is simple and straightforward. I have seen many fantastic teachers who are intuitive in making considered positive changes to the practice. These teachers will continue to perform at a high level without engagement in the activities that I detail here. However, they will improve even more if they become thinking teachers, and reflective practice is essential to that. My argument is that by engaging in reflection, this intuitive development, in terms of a teacher's implicit understanding, will become explicit and deliberate as a model for improvement. By engaging in research and reflective practice, these talented teachers will become more knowledgeable about what works and why, and better informed about the changes they wish to make. They become more confident and develop a greater sense of self-efficacy as teachers. I believe that this self-confidence is essential to a thinking teacher's wellbeing and longevity in their role. My job is to empower you to succeed in the profession. Reflection enables us to take our tacit knowledge, in terms of all the professional learning and experience we naturally draw upon in teaching, and enables us to analyse and synthesise that knowledge as a practical tool.

Unlike Kolb's (1984) reflective theory, Schon (1991) makes a distinction between reflection during an activity as opposed to reflection after the activity. Schon's theory acknowledges reflection in action and reflection on action. This reflection begins with what we already know about our action in the classroom. Consider, for example, the strategies you use to manage the behaviour of the students in your classroom – what do you do to get them to draw their attention to you? It is important to take time to consider what we are currently doing in the classroom and the factors that have informed these approaches. Have we simply employed the strategies that we learned from observing our mentor? What enables these strategies to be effective and what might we want to do to improve them?

Schon's two examples of reflection are worthwhile for you to consider here. What can you do to improve the opportunities you take to reflect while you are teaching, as well as after the lesson is finished? I see reflection in action as a very dynamic process; considering in the moment the effectiveness of the decisions that you are making: why did I ask that particular question? Why did I ask that student to expand upon their answer? Why did I choose that student and ask that particular question? How clear was my explanation or my instructions? This will enable you to find creative, reflective solutions in the moment. Crucially, by engaging in this continual reflection in action, you will become better at it and it will have an even greater impact upon the quality of your teaching and your student outcomes. It becomes a central aspect of the professional practice of the thinking teacher.

Reflection on action can be equally dynamic, but by its very nature it is a more considered type of reflection because of the time available subsequent to the event. By reflecting after the lesson has taken place, you'll be able to spend more time considering all that has happened. You can interpret the various aspects of the lesson and identify what has worked well, as well as considering what changes you wish to make to subsequent lessons as a result. This will impact both upon the outcomes for your students at a whole class level, in terms of the teaching opportunities you design for them. Equally, I find that it has an even greater impact at the individual child level. By engaging in these types of reflection, we are forensically considering the implications of our teaching on each individual student we teach. We are reflecting to consider what we can do differently to improve the learning at this individual student level. As I have said earlier, this is a mindset in that you are relentless in your efforts to enable the learning progress for every student.

2. Action research: experimentation

I will discuss in detail in chapter 4 how your professional learning can be supported by your engagement in action research. At this point, it is just important to acknowledge that active experimentation and engagement in research is a prerequisite for every thinking teacher. However, the extent of this engagement will differ depending on the individual circumstances of each teacher. When I lead a new school, the first thing I will do is to transform the professional environment to ensure that it is as easy as possible for teachers to engage in collaborative action research.

I will encourage every teacher to undertake a master's in education. Being a teacher in England can be demoralising at times because the status afforded to teachers in wider society is not particularly high. I think we should be more highly regarded as professionals, particularly when considering the complexities of our profession. Schools in the UK are usually compared unfavourably with schools in Scandinavia, for example, with Finland widely cited as an education system that we should aspire to. I once asked an education minister from Finland what she considered to be the secret to their success. She laughed and said that it may be due to the fact that they have shorter school days and give less homework! I really can't see those particular strategies going down very well in the UK.

Digging deeper, she explained that the profession certainly enjoys a higher status in Finland, attracting the top graduates. The greatest area of success in Finland, from my perspective, is that the gap between the top schools and the lowest performing schools is one of the narrowest in the world. Research tells us that the greatest factor that impacts on the quality of children's learning experiences in our schools is the quality of teaching. The greatest investment I can make as a school leader, therefore, is in the quality of my teachers' professional learning. Teachers in Finland are expected to engage in research based teaching and every teacher is required to have a master's level degree. This is the greatest investment we can make in our teachers. Approximately 2 to 3% of teachers in the UK have a master's degree. So, not only are we failing to get the best out of our teachers, but also we are not equally encouraging the development of leaders in schools that can effectively support research-based teaching for those they lead or even effectively lead professional learning. As discussed earlier, beyond safeguarding, the leadership of staff learning is my most cherished and greatest responsibility.

Even if one third of the teachers in my schools decide to do an MA, their learning will impact upon their colleagues through the sharing of ideas and strategies. If we encourage a collaborative learning culture, we will take every opportunity possible to learn from each other. For those who don't have the time or inclination to begin an MA, I will provide research summaries for them to read and engage in. I will take every opportunity possible during professional learning meetings to share research. I will use the appraisal system to enable teachers to have research questions as their performance management objectives. Essentially, my job is to create a climate in which teachers see engagement in research as part of their role. As a thinking teacher, you are going to search out opportunities to engage in individual and collaborative action research. This may be an MA, or it may simply involve reading a one-page summary of a research report and trialling a small change to your practice.

3. Peer learning and lesson study

In chapter 4, I will discuss in detail how engagement in peer learning and lesson study will provide regular and powerful professional learning opportunities to engage in reflective practice.

4. Filming/transcripts

Teaching a class of students is an intense activity and there isn't always the opportunity to reflect deeply when you are in the moment. That is why it is important to take opportunities to reflect by putting up a mirror into your classroom. That can be through the eyes of your colleagues, and we will discuss the value of lesson observation later. However, with individuals observing your lesson, there is always the danger that they may move away from authentic reflection into interpretation. An alternative model for you to see your teaching is through the use of recording your lessons, and this can be done through filming or audio transcripts.

Let's start with filming. It can certainly be a strange and uncomfortable experience watching yourself teach. However, once you've overcome this initial discomfort, it is a very useful way to reflect upon your actions and view your teaching from the perspective of your students. Returning to Schon's perspective on reflection on action, filming your lesson enables you to step back from the whirl of general classroom activity and enable you to consider more deeply your decision-making and actions and how they impacted upon your students. This can be done individually or collaboratively. You will begin to notice your physical behaviour in terms of where you place yourself in the classroom and how you may appear to your students. You will be able to analyse the quality of the explanations for example. Filming is also particularly useful when there is a specific aspect of your practice that you wish to investigate.

As a teaching team, we used audio transcripts before we moved onto filming. Audio transcripts enabled us all to gain a reflective window into our classrooms. It enabled us to investigate a key area of our practice in detail, again taking additional time to reflect after the event. In this particular example, as a collective staff team, we were developing our understanding of dialogic teaching (I will share our findings later). We had engaged with the relevant research and were now in a position to experiment and trial changes to our classroom practice. In order to evaluate the impact of these changes, each teacher was asked to undertake a small group activity with five or six students in their classrooms and this group activity was recorded and these recordings were then transcribed. These transcripts were then brought by each individual class teacher to a professional learning meeting after school. The aim for us all was to collectively evaluate our use of questioning and dialogue and the subsequent impact on the learning of our students.

The result was a really powerful learning experience for our teachers. We were able to gain a reflective window into our classroom with some surprising results! Some teachers found they spoke too much or they didn't give sufficient opportunities for children to respond. Others felt that they scaffolded too much, and were too quick to give children the answers. There were many that felt that they gave their students insufficient thinking time to reflect. What we all found was that perhaps we needed to challenge our students more in our questioning. For one particular teacher, this activity was revelatory. She realised that her behaviour was different towards her lower attaining students and those with special educational needs. She had previously always thought she was really positive and supportive of the students. However, when reading her transcript, she realised she was over-praising one child in particular. She would repeatedly say 'well done' without an explanation of what it was exactly that they had done well. Her expectations of this student were not high enough and there was insufficient challenge, and consequently a negative impact on their learning. By reading this transcript and reflecting on the questioning after the lesson, this teacher was then able to make changes to her own behaviour and teaching practice that were implemented immediately. She altered her mindset and her teaching, which I found to be a really powerful example of teacher reflection. As thinking teachers, it is essential that we take every opportunity possible to consider, reflect and think about our teaching and how it impacts on each individual student's learning.

5. Coaching

I have always said that coaching is the most powerful professional learning activity that I engage in. As such, whenever I lead a school, I am determined to ensure that every member of staff is trained as a coach. As a thinking teacher, I urge you to take every opportunity possible to develop your coaching skills. You can do this through being coached and coaching others. In this section I will give you a brief overview of the coaching process and its value to your thinking and professional learning. I have not written this book primarily to provide a practical guide to effective teaching strategies. It has been written to enable you to develop the skills to continually grow and improve. Opportunities for coaching will be crucial to that. If you are in a school in which there may not be a culture for coaching, please seek those opportunities out for yourselves.

Coaching will not only enable you to improve your practice, it will also enable you to develop a solution-focused, reflective mindset. Countless times in this book, I have discussed the fact that teaching is a complex activity. Coaching will give you the time and space to self-assess your teaching practices and find answers to the complex questions you undoubtedly will face. Whether you are considering the learning of a specific group of children, facing a challenging situation with a parent or colleague, or managing your workload, coaching will give you the skills to positively deal with the range of challenges that you will face. I will discuss an example of the coaching process further along. At this point, consider it as a tool to enable you to examine in detail a particular aspect of your practice – an aspect you would like to improve. The job of a coach is to question you in such a way that you are able to examine the situation through a different lens and arrive at potential solutions for yourself. It is very different from the experiences that you may have had through mentoring – your coach is there to empower you, not advise you. The more experience you have of being coached, the more you will become accustomed to asking those questions of yourself and self-coaching. As a thinking teacher, you must aim to develop a positive solution-focused mindset. This will be crucial in enabling you to continue to grow and develop and survive within a challenging profession.

Imagine a coach as a person who 'transports' you from the teacher you currently are and the place you are currently in, to the teacher you aspire to be and the place you want to get to. Coaching will enable you to make quality sustainable change to your practice. It supports the other activities that I encourage through this book and enables you to take the time to deeply reflect upon practice and identify lasting solutions to improve your students' learning outcomes. Coaching is the first professional learning activity that we engage our ECTs in. At an individual level, it is about empowering you to develop the skills to grow for yourself. I have seen many hierarchical leadership systems in schools, in which teachers become disempowered by continually being told what to do, and monitored to check that they are doing it. They then become dependent on affirmation from above; this book is about empowering you to question, reflect, think and learn for yourselves. Almost all the staff I have ever led in schools really enjoy the coaching process and see its benefits. They genuinely look forward to opportunities to be coached.

One model for coaching as an introduction for you is the GROW model, developed by Whitmore (2009) and colleagues in the 1980s. The GROW model comprises four key steps:

Goals: your aspirations

The Goal stage enables you to consider the area of your learning or teaching practice that you may be finding challenging and wish to develop. It enables you to consider your aims. Example questions at this stage may include:

- What do you want to achieve?
- What does success look like for you?
- What makes you feel excited about this goal?
- What would you like to be different when you leave this conversation?

Reality: your current situation in relation to your aspirations

The reality stage is about establishing exactly where you currently are in relation to your learning and teaching. It is about taking the time to reflect upon your current situation, considering what is working well and what you may be finding challenging and why. It is the stage at which the coach can ask questions to clarify your understanding of the current situation. Example questions at this stage may include:

- How would you describe your current situation?
- How are you feeling?
- What is your biggest concern?

Options: the choices and opportunities available to you

The Options stage is about you beginning to consider the range of potential options open to you. It will enable you to reflect on the range of actions you could take, as a prerequisite to consider what you will actually commit to do as a result of the coaching conversation. Example questions at this stage may include:

- What possibilities for action can you currently see?
- If you could start the school year again, what would you do differently?
- What are the advantages and disadvantages of each option?
- How do you feel when you consider each option?

Will: the actions you commit to take to move towards your goals

This stage is about identifying the actions that you have committed to taking. Regular coaching will also ensure that you are more likely to undertake the actions that you have committed to at this stage. Having clarified and developed your understanding of your current situation through your coaching conversation, you have considered the options available to you and identified the key actions for you to move forward. Crucially, you have arrived at the actions for yourself, therefore you own them. You haven't been given any direct advice or instruction. Example questions at this stage may include:

- On a scale of one to 10, how committed and motivated are you to completing this action? What would take you to a 10?
- What is your first step?
- What will success look like and feel like to you?

Coaching can only take place within a culture of high trust and respect. You will not be likely to authentically open up your practice as a teacher if you feel that you cannot trust your coach. So, the relationship between you and your coach will be crucial to your learning and development. I did not discover coaching until my fourth year of teaching. I immediately felt the benefits and it is something I will continue to engage with throughout my career. That is why I am sharing this approach with you; the sooner you begin to experience coaching in your career, the better. All the staff I work with have become more creative and reflective through coaching. When faced with challenges, they are more likely to seek to identify solutions rather than have a 'moan'. Through coaching, the aim is for you to be empowered to continually question, reflect and improve. It is as much about identifying your strengths as it is considering the areas for improvement. If you are unable to access regular coaching consider opportunities that are available to you to use the GROW approach to self-coach yourselves. If you can find a willing colleague to support you in this process, even better. However, do not underestimate the power and value of regular engagement in coaching.

6. Appreciative enquiry

Appreciative enquiry is a form of coaching and I will discuss it in greater detail in chapter 4.

7. Collaborative professional dialogue/planning

It remains the case that, in too many schools, teachers continue to work and learn in isolation in their classrooms. During my doctoral research, I found that the most valued professional learning activity shared by participants was collaboration with colleagues. Teachers want to work with others and to discuss their ideas and teaching, and not necessarily in a hierarchical relationship such as a mentor for ECTs, or a professional tutor for trainee teachers. Teachers want to be able to work with others in a collaborative supportive way. That is why I always try to create as many opportunities as possible for teachers to learn and work in collaboration with their peers. Examples include collaborative planning, collaborative action research, peer learning and lesson study. The more opportunities we get to work with others, within a culture of high trust, the more opportunities we get to engage in authentic professional dialogue with each other. For thinking teachers, engagement in authentic collaborative professional dialogue is essential to our growth and development.

I was recently asked during a podcast, 'What advice would I give to teachers who are working within a school in which collaboration or creativity isn't encouraged?' An example provided to me was of teachers in the United States who were given a script to teach from. In this example, evaluators are then employed to ensure that teachers are not straying from the script. The first thought that came to my mind was why would anyone choose to stifle teachers in such a way? How can we expect to nurture creative, critical thinking in our students if we are not encouraging a similar environment for our teachers? My response was to urge teachers to search out collaborative learning opportunities for themselves. Take every opportunity you can to work alongside like-minded peers to discuss your planning, teaching and student outcomes. Collaboration is key to your professional learning and development and, most importantly, it will impact positively on your students' learning outcomes.

8. Observing others/being observed

Watching others teach, or allowing others to watch you, are both valuable opportunities to think, reflect and consider your teaching practice. However, I believe it is crucial that it is not undertaken in a judgemental way – the focus cannot be on grading/judging the lesson. Instead, it must focus on learning and therefore needs to be undertaken within a culture of high challenge and high trust. It can be organised within a mentoring capacity, in which you observe or are observed by a more experienced teacher. However, it is crucial that you have opportunities for reflection. For example, when observing a skilled and experienced teacher, take the opportunity to question their strategies and decision making. What are the underlying assumptions and knowledge that informs their decision making? Take opportunities to reflect upon what changes you may wish to make to your own practice as a consequence of your observations and reflections. Take time to consider the specific aspects of practice you are looking to observe and consider. I will often ask teachers to demonstrate key aspects of their teaching practice for others, for example 'guided reading'. This can potentially include an entire staff team watching a single teacher teaching a 'model lesson'.

Equally, when you are being observed, ensure that it is a collaborative learning experience in which the outcome is a professional learning conversation that enables you to consider, think and reflect upon your practice. Take time to communicate to your observer prior to the observation the specific aspects of your practice that you wish to develop or have been experimenting with. Most teachers I have met in my career have found lesson observations to be quite a pressurised or even stressful process (I would argue that there are very few professions in which observation of practice is conducted in such a judgemental way). It is not as easy for us to be our authentic selves when we feel stressed or under pressure, and this will hinder the learning process and the quality of the professional dialogue. This is especially true if we feel we cannot be honest and open. I would like the practice of being observed teaching to be seen as a luxurious process, in which professional colleagues support you in your reflections. Ultimately, they are providing a reflective lens to support your learning, growth and development.

There remains too great a focus in schools on lesson observations that are used to grade and judge teachers. These 'judgemental lesson observations' usually take place within a power relationship in which the teacher feels the experience is 'done to them' rather than 'with them'. As discussed earlier, once you know the experience is primarily for judgement rather than learning, you are more likely to play safe and less likely to experiment and take risks. As thinking teachers, taking risks and trialling changes is part of our mindset as creative, active, reflective practitioners. We never use lesson observations to make or provide judgements of our teachers (in England over many years, we have judged our teachers on a continuum from 'outstanding' to 'inadequate'). We value our teachers taking creative risks during lesson observations because we believe, subsequently, more potential learning will take place.

When lesson observations are not being graded or judged, teachers tend to become more comfortable in opening up and discussing their own and each other's practice. Rather than seeing themselves as being in competition with their colleagues, they are more likely to collaborate with and actively seek out the opinions of their colleagues. We have found that teachers are more likely to approach each other and take time to visit each other's classrooms for valuable informal learning opportunities too. In our education system, there remains a dominant culture in which teachers continue to work in isolation. We need to encourage a culture of collaborative learning, driven by practitioners. The negative legacy of judgemental lesson observations can also mean that it can sometimes take longer for more experienced colleagues to adapt to a culture of openness and challenge through collaborative peer learning observations.

9. Student voice

I have discussed previously how our interpretation of the impact of our teaching on the success of an individual lesson can differ from the perceptions of our students. Ultimately, our teaching should be judged quite simply in terms of its impact on the learning outcomes of the students that we teach. When I write about 'learning outcomes', I am not referring solely to academic outcomes in terms of test results/grades. I am also referring to our impact upon their social, emotional and personal growth and development.

If we view student outcomes as the ultimate barometer to measure the quality of our teaching, we cannot be authentic thinking teachers if we don't value the thoughts, perceptions and opinions of our students. Put simply, student voice must be at the centre of our teaching. Take every opportunity possible to ensure that your students also have opportunities to think, reflect and share their understandings. This does not mean that they are given opportunities to judge the quality of your teaching; it means they are given opportunities as often as possible to share and discuss the quality of their learning! For a thinking teacher, these opportunities form a significant part of the reflective process. By understanding the learning needs of your students, you will be in a stronger position to adapt your teaching and challenge them in a continuous cycle of improvement. In chapter 5, I will discuss the value of assessment for learning, dialogic teaching and metacognitive questioning in enabling you to develop a learning environment in your classroom that will encourage all your students to thrive as learners. At this point, I will set the scene by giving you three examples of questions that you can use to support you to develop your students' metacognition. Consider the typical expectations for dialogue in your classroom. Consider the extent to which you currently use questions such as these in your current practice:

1. How do you know when you have learned something?

2. When you find something tricky, what do you do to help yourself?
3. How do you feel when you learn something new?

10. Self-questioning/learning journals

I'm sure that you will have realised that at the heart of a thinking teacher is a commitment to self-questioning and self-reflection. I think that most teachers engage in a form of self-questioning and reflection. Often however, we do very little with this self-questioning and reflection. However, as thinking teachers, we are making an active commitment to using self-questioning and reflective practice to make refinements and improvements to our practice. The purpose of engaging in master's level study is to give you opportunities to take time to consider and question your practice. Crucially, it gives you the additional opportunity to articulate and synthesise your thoughts on paper through written assignments. I find writing to be an essential skill in enabling me to collect, order and organise my thinking and learning. It enables me to feel safe in knowing that my self-questioning and reflections won't simply be lost in the ether!

So, I would urge you as thinking teachers to keep and maintain a learning journal. The first thing that I did as a headteacher was to encourage the use of learning journals for all members of staff. These journals will enable you to keep a written record of your reflections and this will support you in both your current and future learning. I find the writing process to be a thinking and learning activity in itself. Through the process of writing, we are taking the time to synthesise our thinking. The journal will offer a fantastic way in which you can record your ongoing reflections and learning and it is a really good habit for you to develop in your first year of teaching. By recording these reflections in your journal, you will be able to track your learning and the impact of the changes that you are making to your practice and the learning of your students.

The current picture . . .

In the next chapter, I will share some of the findings from my own doctoral research, particularly in terms of teachers' experiences of professional learning in our schools. You will know how passionate I am about the value of teacher learning, particularly in terms of the direct impact that this has on our students' learning outcomes. You know that I believe leaders in school should take responsibility in developing an expansive learning environment in our schools that encourages formal and informal teacher professional learning activities. I do believe that teacher experiences of professional learning have improved during my career. However, I still believe that the pace of this improvement remains too slow and the professional learning experiences of too many teachers in our schools remains inadequate. As discussed earlier, latest figures in England show that 25% of teachers leave the profession within their first three years of teaching. Among newly qualified teachers, the number who left within their first year rose from 11.7% in 2020 to 12.5% in 2021 (Belger, 2022). This is not acceptable. I have written this book to empower you to influence the learning environment around you and to take charge of your own learning and development.

A report of the School Improvement Commission entitled 'Improving Schools' (November 2020) detailed the ambition to build a school system of high excellence and high equity. In relation to school leadership, they discovered the need for school leaders to create the conditions in which teachers can succeed. What they found was leaders who were driven more by a need to be ready for Ofsted Inspections rather than a focus on improving teaching and learning. They reported that too many schools were focused on quick fix approaches rather than sustainable school improvement over time. We remain entrenched within an education system that is too highly focused on competition at both school and teacher level, rather than collaboration. The first recommendation made in the report is specifically related to teacher learning:

1. Every school should prioritise staff development and designate a senior leader as the professional development lead who is responsible for overseeing, coordinating and championing high-quality teacher professional development.

I would go further and say that it should be the responsibility of the headteacher to lead teacher professional learning.

The research is detailing the value of collaborative professional learning in impacting positively on student outcomes but practice in our schools is not reflecting this. As Gandhi said, 'Be the change you want to see'. I believe that my leadership of a thinking school has demonstrated my commitment to 'being' and enabling the change that I would like to see at a national level in the three schools in which I have had the privilege of being headteacher. In the final line of my first book, *The Thinking School*, I outlined my ambition to move from a thinking school to a thinking schools system. One move towards that is this book and my invitation to you to be the change that you want to see in your school!

An OECD (2015) report that looked at schools across Europe, entitled 'Schools for 21st-Century Learners', made the following recommendations:

- Empower teachers to play a role in decision-making at the whole school level.
- Provide opportunities for and remove barriers to professional learning for principals.
- Principals need to focus on teaching and learning.
- Strengthen teachers' confidence.
- Encourage collaboration among teachers.

The reason I am sharing this wider picture at this point in the book is to demonstrate that there remains work to be done. By empowering yourself as a thinking teacher, you will develop your self-efficacy and your self-confidence. Through collaboration, you will influence the expansiveness of the learning environment around you. Through reflective practice, you will develop the skills to continually think and continually learn and grow. This will have a powerful impact on your own professional learning and wellbeing and, most importantly, on the learning of the students that you teach. With this positive and learning-focused mindset, you will also influence many other teachers, and consequently students, throughout your career.

Summary

In this third chapter, I have detailed how we are working in a highly complex profession and how we will undoubtedly face many challenges. By becoming thinking teachers, we develop a mindset and commitment to engage in deep reflective professional learning activities within a cycle of continual learning and improvement. We do this because it will enable us to meet and overcome the challenges we face in a positive learning-focused way. In the following chapter, I will provide a more detailed overview of the value to thinking teachers of engagement in action research, peer learning and lesson study.

Relevant reading

Belger, T. (2022) 'Jump in teachers leaving, plus 6 more school workforce findings', *SchoolsWeek*, 9 June.

Dewey, J. (1933) *How We Think: A Restatement of the Relation of Reflective Thinking to the Educative Process.* Boston, MA: D.C. Heath & Co Publishers.

Gibbs, G. (1988) Learning by Doing: A guide to teaching and learning methods. Further Education Unit. Oxford Polytechnic: Oxford.

Kolb, D. A. (1984) Experiential learning: experience as the source of learning and development. Englewood Cliffs, NJ: Prentice Hall.

Kolb, D. A. and Fry, R. (1975) Toward an Applied Theory of Experiential Learning. In Cooper, C., Ed., *Theories of Group Process*, John Wiley, 33-57.

OECD (2015) Schools for 21st-Century Learners: Strong Leaders, Confident Teachers, Innovative Approaches. International Summit on the Teaching Profession. Paris: OECD Publishing.

Schleicher, A. (2015) *Schools for 21st century learners: strong leaders, confident teachers, innovative approaches.* Paris: OECD Publishing.

Schon, D. (1991) *The Reflective Practitioner - how professionals think in action.* Aldershot: Ashgate.

School Improvement Commission (November 2020) Improving Schools. London: National Assosciation of Head Teachers.

Reflective questions

1. To what extent do you feel comfortable in taking risks and trialling changes in your practice?
2. What opportunities do you currently have to engage in reflective practice?

3. What opportunities would you like to take next to support your professional learning and reflective practice?

4. Who could support you in your development of reflective practice?

5. What barriers exist currently for you in relation to the previous questions? What steps could you take to overcome these barriers?

Chapter 4

Activities for Thinking Teachers

Action research

I encourage all the teachers I work with to engage in action research. The primary reason for this is that it provides a framework for us as thinking teachers to support our reflective practice. In this book, I will focus on action research as a research methodology simply because my doctoral research investigated teacher engagement in action research. Therefore, I can share with you what participants saw as the challenges and benefits of action research. However, I would urge you to participate in any form of practitioner research that you deem to be most appropriate. I would advocate that you engage in research because it will enable you to develop your knowledge, skills and understanding of teaching, and crucially, to improve your practice. Having shared my own learning journey with you in this book, you will understand how much I have benefitted from undertaking research in my own classrooms and schools. Action research will support your reflective practice as thinking teachers. As a cyclical model of learning, it relates very well to the models of reflective practice I presented in the previous chapter.

One of the core values of action research is that it supports 'learning over time'. Reviews of teacher professional learning (see Cordingley et al, 2015; GTCE, 2007) demonstrate that teacher learning is still not sufficiently sustained over time. In addition, it is not likely to be evidence based, with insufficient choice for teachers. When supporting teachers to engage in action research, I will ensure that they always have opportunities to select the focus for their research. We may be focussing on overarching whole-school topics (I will share some examples of this in the next chapter) but it is essential that teachers get the opportunity to decide the focus for their study. Action research is the methodology I deploy for our teachers because its design equips them with practical methods for developing knowledge from their experiences in the classroom. Action research has developed from the work of Stenhouse (1975), whose model of 'teacher as researcher' revolved around enabling teachers to value the importance of lifelong learning. The literature on action research clearly emphasises the researcher actively participating in the study and investigating changes to their practice. For this reason, it relates very well to your role as thinking teachers.

Engagement in action research should be seen as a central component of your role as a teacher. Your role as a researcher is to intentionally change and improve your teaching and its impact on your students' learning. Unlike other research methodologies, you are not necessarily looking to generate new theories. Your research will be valued more in terms of its impact on improving your own (and others') practice. It is about enabling your reflective research skills to continually improve. Action research will equip you with the design tools to find solutions to the most complex questions you will face in your classroom. Put simply, you identify a research question that you wish to investigate, in relation to your classroom practice. You then undertake relevant reading and consider an action or actions that you wish to investigate. Through reflection and evaluation, you then determine the impact of those actions on your students' learning experiences. As a result of your findings, you then make the necessary adjustments to your future practice.

Action research is not a methodology exclusive to teachers. However, it is a popular methodology for teacher researchers. A few researchers

(Mcniff and Whitehead, 2005: Elliot, 2007) have adapted action research to define a methodology specifically designed for teachers to undertake research within their own education settings. Similar to my exploration of reflective practice in chapter 3, they have investigated the use of cyclical models for learning through action research, which involve you as teacher researcher in planning, reflecting, observing, revising and then repeating the cycle. This model of action research promotes a process of action and reflection designed to improve your practice. I advocate it for you as thinking teachers because you don't have to have a research background to participate. As defined in this chapter, it enables you to learn about your teaching in your classroom to improve your practice.

To finish this section, I will illustrate an example of a teacher I worked with who benefitted greatly from engagement in action research. In the school where I have been headteacher for ten years, over 80% of the teachers currently in class joined our school as student teachers. I believe that the quality of the learning environment for staff in your schools should be measured through the eyes of the latest entrant – the student teacher or the early career teacher. As a thinking school, we expect every member of staff to benefit from a really expansive learning environment and as such, we expect them all to engage in collaborative action research. An individual's development as a thinking teacher is continual and ongoing. As soon as a student teacher enters our school, we expect them to feel the benefit of the range of professional learning activities I share in this book.

I will share an example of a student teacher who arrived on a placement in a challenging year 6 class in the first term of my third year of headship. As I was teaching in year 6 at the time, I was able to regularly (informally) observe this teacher in action. Not just in the classroom, but in her interactions with children and colleagues beyond the classroom, for example during professional learning meetings and collaborative planning sessions. Remember how in chapter 2, I discussed the importance of non-judgemental (lesson) observations and the value of encouraging a learning mentality, as opposed to a performance mentality. If anyone had seen her teaching in that first term, they would not have been particularly impressed. She was very raw as a teacher, and one of her mentors at the time (who was not a thinking teacher) actually warned me about her lack of behaviour management skills. Again, notice how some teachers are so quick to judge others. At the time however, I wasn't as interested in her teaching capabilities as much as I was in her attitudes and dispositions to her own learning.

We appointed her as a teacher at our school for the following September. In fact, we placed her in year 6, which is widely regarded by many in the profession (not myself, all classes and age groups are important and challenging) as the most important year group in primary schools. In fact, at the time, colleagues on her course questioned her headteacher's sanity for making such a decision. This was a particularly challenging year to be teaching in year 6 because we all had to adapt to the implementation of a new curriculum and assessment framework. As with all newly qualified teachers, we encouraged her to begin her master's degree in her first term of teaching and she did so with great enthusiasm. She was aware of her own strengths, in particular her ability to form excellent learning relationships with her students. She was also very open about the many areas of her practice that she needed to develop. Through engagement in action research, she was able to lead her own professional learning and engage in sustained learning activities over time. She was and remains to this day a great example of a thinking teacher.

To cut a long story short, this particular teacher completed her MA in education before the end of her third year of teaching and was appointed as year group leader in year 6. For each of her three years of teaching in year 6, student learning outcomes placed the school in the top 6% of schools in London for pupil progress. By giving her the time, space and opportunities to think, learn and grow, she was able to develop from that 'raw' student teacher to a highly reflective, confident, highly skilled thinking teacher. I often wonder how many teachers we lose from our profession each year because they were never afforded the same learning opportunities.

The development of action research as a tool to support teacher learning

As you will have become aware, I have always been interested in teacher professional learning, and in particular teacher engagement in research. My aim as a school leader has been to make it as easy as possible for teachers to undertake research in their classrooms, and that is where the model of action research fits in. A 2007 study jointly commissioned by the General Teaching Council of England (GTCE) and the Association of Teachers and Lecturers (ATL) aimed to summarise the different research and evaluation reports that had been commissioned by government agencies to evaluate teachers' professional learning. Their findings concluded that effective teacher learning involved:

1. Sustained interactions and interventions (as opposed to individual training sessions)

2. Teacher choice and influence over their professional development

3. Activities designed to take account of the individual needs and priorities of teachers at different stages of their professional lives and careers.

4. Collaborative work within a professional learning community

I am referring to it because it remains relevant today. Consider for a moment the four key findings detailed above and reflect on the extent to which the school environment you are currently working in enables teachers to: engage in sustained learning activities over time; define and influence their own professional learning; experience personalised professional learning activities directly related to their current stage of learning/development; be a part of a wider collaborative professional learning community. A further review of teacher professional learning (Cordingley et al, 2015) demonstrated that teacher learning has continued to be insufficiently sustained over time or evidence-based and with a lack of teacher choice. Sounds very familiar.

The other reason that I have presented these research findings is that they relate so closely to the model of action research that I present for you in this chapter. The research is telling us what effective professional learning looks like, so why do we not see this reflected more consistently in our schools? Whenever I lead a new school, my experience is that teachers have become used to experiencing one-off professional development sessions after school each week that reflects a one-size-fits-all methodology. For you to be a thinking teacher, I need you to actively consider your own professional development needs and to ensure that the professional learning activities you engage in take into account your current knowledge and skills and challenge you to learn and improve – in the same way that I would expect your teaching activities to do for your students. I want you to engage in professional learning activities that are sustained over time and I expect you to work in collaboration with your colleagues. Engagement in collaborative action research will support you to do this.

I advocate action research as a methodology for teacher inquiry because its design equips teachers with practical methods to develop knowledge from their experience in classrooms. Action research has been presented by a number of writers as an effective methodology for teacher professional learning, enabling learning in the school environment about the school environment to develop and change practice (for examples, see Kemmis, 2010; Mcniff and Whitehead, 2005; Somekh, 1998; and Lomax, 2002). I believe that there have traditionally been insufficient opportunities for teachers to engage in research. Remember that every teacher in Finland is expected to have a master's degree. In the UK, approximately 2-3% of teachers have a master's degree. There remains insufficient encouragement for teacher research, and the wider education system does not support it. Billet (2001) has argued how the system of inspection and statutory measures do not support the development and adoption of action research by teachers. I would go further and argue that the pressures on school leaders encourage the implementation of one-off staff training sessions, at the expense of activities that require engagement in deeper learning over time. Teachers are not given the space and time they need to explore their practice. The pressures on our teachers need to be considered and we continue to see vast numbers leave the profession each year. As a thinking teacher, you will need to actively take responsibility for your own professional learning.

Stenhouse's (1975) model of a teacher as a researcher is very much about teachers valuing the importance of lifelong learning and he is considered by many to be the foremost proponent of action research in schools. Different education researchers may present slightly adapted models of action research. However, there is a clear emphasis in all the literature on action research on action, change and researcher as participant. Your role as action researcher is, therefore, to set out to improve the situation that you are studying. You are studying your classroom and your students. The yardstick for measuring the outcomes of your research is not in terms of the theories you come up with, but in terms of the changes you make to your practice. Mills (2003) has stressed the distinction of action research as research undertaken specifically for themselves, to attain personal learning and support pupil learning, and Saunders (2007) has discussed how significant this teacher research is in enabling researchers to find answers within local contexts. The knowledge you are creating as a teacher researcher is far more meaningful because it is created in the very context (your classroom) where it will continue to be used and developed. The model I am presenting of action research is a cyclical one that will involve you in planning, reflecting, observing, reviewing and then repeating the cycle. By engaging in action research, you are learning in the school environment about the school environment to develop and change your practice. Action research is flexible enough to ensure that, as thinking teachers, you do not need to have a research background to be able to engage in research.

Impact of action research

As part of my doctoral research, I read and analysed a multitude of research papers/journals/books to identify the potential impact on teachers and their students of engagement in action research. I needed to do this because my personal experience in schools had demonstrated to me that there are clearly barriers in place that stifle teacher engagement in research. I knew that many teachers did not engage in research, and this was primarily because of a lack of knowledge or a lack of time and support. All the research studies I read detailed the positive impact of engaging in action research on teachers' professional knowledge and skills. In this section I will detail the key factors involved in the process of action research that are particularly significant in the development of this professional knowledge and skills.

One significant factor for teachers was how action research enabled opportunities for collaborative working/learning with other professionals within and beyond the school. Models of collaboration varied, but of particular significance in many of these studies was the value placed by teachers of opportunities for professional dialogue. This cannot be underestimated. You must ensure that you are making and taking as many opportunities as possible to engage in collaborative professional dialogue. Collaboration was seen as pivotal in empowering teachers to become more open about their practice, an aspect that can often be indirectly discouraged through many of the mechanisms in place in schools. For example, performance related pay or judgemental/graded lesson observations within hierarchical school cultures that have an overemphasis on monitoring and compliance. In contrast, a number of studies highlighted the value of peer support and peer observation and learning in particular, as critical to teacher learning. Peer learning is also a key component in the development of a professional learning community, particularly in terms of its distinction as a model from teachers' previous experiences of observations with leaders/managers, which have predominantly been focused on performance and judgements as opposed to learning and supportive development. The BERA-RSA (2014) report on the role of research in teacher education highlighted the value to successful professional learning of collaborative enquiry and structured peer support. I do believe that the picture has improved in recent years. There is a greater emphasis in schools on peer learning and even Ofsted have moved away from graded lesson observations in recent years. However, we still see too many teachers leave the profession and a lack of expansive professional learning opportunities for teachers in schools. That is why it remains so important for you, as thinking teachers, to take charge of your own learning.

Whether or not your school provides an environment that enables teacher engagement in research, you need to take opportunities for yourself to engage in reflective practice/action research. I arrived at my first school as a rookie headteacher with a grand plan to ensure that every teacher had the opportunity to engage in collaborative action research within their year group teams over the duration of my first term. Just weeks prior to me arriving, the school had experienced an unsuccessful

Ofsted inspection, in which the school had been judged to be 'requiring improvement'. I inherited a teaching team who were extremely low on morale, having basically been told that they weren't good enough! They were working incredibly hard but were not seeing this hard work reflected in student outcomes. The leadership structure at the school had been extremely hierarchical and teachers complied with the demands made by school leaders without question. I strongly felt that engagement in collaborative action research would enable these enthusiastic teachers (many of whom were relatively inexperienced) to have the time and space to develop their practice.

Although I have discussed this experience earlier in the book, I think it is worthwhile to examine this further at this point, particularly in relation to the value of engagement in action research. As a 'requiring improvement' school, you are placed under considerable pressure by the local authority (LA) to demonstrate rapid improvement, and we were subject to additional visits from the LA appointed school improvement partner (SIP). When I first met her, she informed me that I needed to move the school forward and asked me how I planned to do this. I explained to her that I was halfway through my doctoral research and that I had a great plan! I went on to explain to her that I planned for all teachers to engage in collaborative action research projects within their year group teams and that this would take the entire term (13 school weeks). We were to focus on the research of Professor Paul Black and Dylan Wiliam and their work on assessment for learning. Each year group would read the research and decide upon their own research question in relation to the context of the cohorts of students in their individual year groups. They would each use the action research cycle to trial changes and make improvements to their practice. There would be no graded lesson observations and instead, all teachers would participate in peer learning activities. I was determined to give them the time and space to learn, reflect and grow – to actively begin their journey to becoming thinking teachers. I explained that at the end of term, we would hold a celebration session in which each year group team would share their findings. These findings would then be collated and would be written up in a document entitled, 'Assessment for Learning and Teaching Policy' – this document would represent our co-constructed collective reflective roadmap to improvement for our school.

Now, I was quite pleased with my plan – what do you think of it? You can guess what the response of our SIP was. Let's just say that she wasn't quite as enthusiastic about it as I was. In fact, she explained that action research was not an appropriate model for teacher development for a school in our position, that it was a more appropriate professional learning tool for 'outstanding' schools. She wanted me to undertake judgemental lesson observations of every teacher and to grade them according to a four-point scale of outstanding, good, requiring improvement or inadequate. As I stated before, who exactly would be motivated by being labelled as 'inadequate'? It doesn't really provide much impetus to your professional confidence. There was no mention of collaboration at all. This is not a personal criticism, but this particular SIP was also the LA lead for teacher continuing professional development (CPD) – it is merely a reflection of the low expectations for teacher professional learning that are entrenched within our education system. Her views clearly reflected the expectations of school leadership and teacher learning in England at the time (2012). She also explained that if we didn't manage to get the school to improve its judgement at its next Ofsted Inspection in approximately 18 months, I could lose my job.

I could easily have abandoned my philosophy for teacher learning and school improvement, but I would have been working in a way that wasn't aligned with my personal and professional values and beliefs and I certainly would not be writing this book right now. I made the decision to ignore her advice and to stick with my original plan. I hope that you have seen through this book that thinking teachers are values led and research-informed, and they understand why it is important to be this way. They think, they question and they challenge. Needless to say, those same teachers who were told that they were either inadequate or requiring improvement (basically written off as not good enough) were the same teachers informed by Ofsted just a few years later that they were outstanding. At the end of that first term, I asked the teachers to reflect on their professional learning experiences. I have shared some of their responses for you:

The learning opportunities helped me reflect on my teaching strategies that support the needs of my learners. The reflections have been effective in helping me realise that certain strategies are not as effective as others.

Peer learning has been great. As a NQT I am not as confident in various aspects of teaching as more experienced teachers. Having the time to have discussions with colleagues about techniques to try in my class or ways to really make sure all children are progressing has been really beneficial.

I have found peer learning and action research to be very successful and useful. I was able to learn a lot about my own practice. It also gave me the time to reflect and evaluate my own practice through discussions with others in my team.

It has been really beneficial to have peer learning opportunities and to understand about reflective practice and action research. It has made me more open to being observed and rather than seeing it as an opportunity for criticism, I now see it as a development opportunity. I liked how we were given academic literature and given time to read it.

Relating to the research studies detailed earlier, engagement in action research enabled teachers to demystify areas of their practice, and they felt that they had developed both their professional and personal skills. There was a direct impact upon teachers' strategies in the classroom, as they overcame long-held beliefs and made changes to their practice. I ask teachers to engage in action research because it makes them more confident and autonomous. In becoming thinking teachers, they are continually reflecting upon the impact of their teaching on student outcomes. Action research encourages and forces you to reflect and make changes to your practice. This then has the effect of enabling you to become more autonomous in your professional judgements. Many of the studies highlighted teachers' perceptions that engaging in action research enhanced their self-confidence. Remember that teaching is a tough job, so self-confidence and autonomy are crucial factors in supporting our wellbeing. The most common underlying theme in the research is the assertion that teachers' views changed about different aspects of teaching and learning and their beliefs around the role of the teacher, and they became both more confident in their own judgements and in themselves.

I have always wanted teachers to engage in action research because I want them to move away from the factors over which they have no control to focus on those that they do. Consider action research to be a structured way in which you can engage in reflective practice cycles, as discussed in chapter 3. In addition to the reflective practice cycle described, you explicitly engage in research to support your learning and to improve your practice. We may have limited power in impacting upon the socio-economic or cultural factors that could be affecting our students' learning or aspirations. Often, we can fall into the trap of making excuses for pupil underachievement, and we can associate these factors as related to disadvantage. Action research enables us to focus on the environment in which we can make a real difference – our classrooms and our schools. Once your students cross the threshold into your classroom/school, you have the power to make a positive difference. Your job is to empower your students to believe that they can achieve. They will internalise the expectations you hold for them. Teaching is a great job so never forget the positive difference that you can make. Action research enables you to reflect on your practice and make the timely changes that you need to make. This will make the greatest difference on those students that otherwise may not succeed in the school setting.

One person once told me that children learn more between the ages of zero and three than at any other time in their lives. They learn to walk and can communicate in multiple languages if the environment supports it. Consider how many times a child falls whilst learning to walk. They may learn to walk at different rates, but all children get there eventually. They are consciously aware that through effort they will succeed. Children are creative, imaginative, resilient and innate learners. Are these skills reflected successfully in your classroom or your school? For many children, the first time they begin to doubt themselves as learners is when they come to school and receive feedback from adults. As thinking teachers, reflect carefully on your actions and how they impact upon the extent to which your students can develop their learning skills.

Peer learning

When I first became a headteacher, I inherited a teaching team that I could see was filled with fear and anxiety when faced with lesson observations. For these teachers, lesson observations were primarily focused on 'performing' rather than 'learning'. Judgemental lesson observations are observations in which teachers are graded and set targets for improvement. As discussed earlier, this encourages a culture of playing safe rather than taking risks or engaging in deep reflection. I really felt that we needed to move away from a culture of hierarchical judgemental lesson observations in favour of a model that focused on collaborative professional dialogue. I wanted teachers to direct and drive their own learning and to decide upon the areas of focus that they needed to develop. Newly qualified and student teachers are far more likely to express their areas for development because they see this as an important part of their role as students/early career teachers. I would like you to take this mindset, as thinking teachers, and maintain it throughout your career. To continue to be open and challenge yourself to identify areas for growth and development. I would urge you to participate in peer learning whenever possible and, in this section, I will discuss the ways in which you can organise this.

You will know by now how much I advocate collaborative professional dialogue and learning, and I think it is something that doesn't happen often enough in our schools. From a very simple perspective, I know that myself and my colleagues will have our own individual strengths. By working together, we can combine these individual strengths within a culture of collaborative collective improvement. We could each be doing well individually, but by working together we each have the potential to improve. I share this with our staff team by emphasising the value of collaboration and combined wisdom as crucial to our continual improvement as thinking teachers. By regularly engaging in peer learning, we iron out our individual differences and build greater consistency in our teaching practice. This does not mean that everyone teaches in exactly the same way; it means that everyone is willing to improve and to deploy the best possible teaching strategies.

I often hear the term 'consistency' being used by school leaders, and frequently in a misappropriated way. For example, leaders may encourage consistency of practice by determining that all teachers within a year group team teach the same lesson in the same way at the same time, or to organise their classroom environments in exactly the same way. However, this 'consistency' may not necessarily reflect or meet the learning of the students in that classroom. I prefer to get teams to focus on 'consistency of outcomes'. We agree on what we want the outcomes for our students to be – we may say that we wish to have limitless expectations of our students learning outcomes and that we want to enable them to become motivated, creative, independent, critical thinkers. We are both energetic and relentless in working towards these goals. I prefer this model of consistency in which our beliefs, values and aims are aligned. However, how these goals are achieved will differ dependent upon the individual class and individual student. We are consistent in ensuring that all of our teachers engage in expansive, personalised professional learning opportunities and this will include opportunities for collaborative professional learning.

Peer learning is practitioner led and, therefore, ideal for thinking teachers. In peer learning, one teacher observes another and provides feedback on what they saw through a reflective professional learning conversation. It doesn't have to be restricted to two teachers either and we have found it useful to organise it in trios as we are a three-form entry school. The greater the number of people that are involved, the more reflective and diverse the learning conversation can be. If you are the teacher being observed, you are in charge of identifying the area of focus that you would like your peer(s) to reflect upon. This area of focus may be an area of your practice that you are specifically seeking to develop, or you may be looking at a new strategy that is being implemented at a whole school or year group level. It is imperative that this dialogue takes place within a culture of mutual trust. If so, it will be a fantastic experience for all involved. If peer learning is not a strategy that is embedded in your school, take your own opportunities where possible to engage in the practice with your colleagues. In the first instance, you may want to choose a like-minded colleague with whom you have already established a productive working relationship.

Peer learning enables self-evaluation and development and offers first-hand experience and direct evidence about what happens in other classrooms. Reflection is a core activity to the thinking teacher and peer learning is a valuable activity in both supporting you to reflect on your own practice, as well as enjoying the luxury of reflecting upon the practice of others. It is a frustration of mine that, generally, teachers get insufficient opportunities to watch others teach, when I know it is such a valuable learning opportunity. When first undertaking peer learning, it is important that you stick to a disciplined structure that will enable all participants to maximise the learning experience. You do not want it to be a general lesson observation with a lack of sufficient focus. You really need to ensure that you have agreed the specific area of focus that all participants will be reflecting upon, and you need to ensure that the observers are not distracted from this focus area into looking at other areas of practice. Peer learning offers a means by which teachers can deepen their awareness and understanding of the following:

- What goes on in their classrooms.
- The impact of their interactions in the classroom.
- Their own and their pupils' learning.

I hope you can see how well it relates to the model of reflective practitioner presented in chapter 3.

The impact will be even more powerful if all the teachers in your school are engaging. It enables assessment for learning processes to have an impact on your own learning; it puts you in control of your own learning, allowing you to start from where you are and challenges you, within an environment of professional safety, to improve. Peer learning encourages colleagues to engage in professional dialogue with a specific focus on student outcomes and will support the wider teaching team to develop a 'shared language' about teacher learning. This will also impact positively on the wider school culture. To develop a belief that, as a team, we see the importance of actively opening up our practice and engaging in professional learning conversations with a specific focus on our students' learning outcomes. The greater the number of teachers that are engaging, the greater the number of practitioners that you can learn with and from.

I could relay countless examples in the schools that I have led on the impact on teachers of engagement in peer learning. Remember that there must be a culture of mutual trust for it to be successful. Once that is established, I can tell you that it is an experience that teachers really enjoy participating in, as long as they are confident that their practice isn't going to be 'judged'. Feedback from teachers has demonstrated that they certainly see it as a more powerful professional learning activity than the typical experiences of hierarchical judgemental lesson observations. So many of our practices at our school have been established because of our regular engagement in peer learning. It has supported us in establishing our overarching teaching pedagogy of dialogic teaching across the school. I will discuss the value of dialogic teaching further in chapter 5 and I would expect every thinking teacher to have a strong understanding of dialogic teaching strategies. When we were first establishing it at our school, we used peer learning as the vehicle through which we would trial changes to our practice and develop our understanding of what works well and why – through these experiences we learned so much.

For example, we realised that too often teachers were dominating the classroom discussion and not allowing sufficient opportunities for children to build upon the ideas of others. Teachers were intervening and responding to every comment made by their students because this had become part of their established practice. We found and agreed that, as teachers, we also responded too quickly, giving insufficient 'thinking time' to students. This was a real eye-opener for our teachers and thinking time quickly and easily became embedded as a key strategy across our school. This was as a direct result of us visiting each other's classrooms and then engaging in honest, authentic professional dialogue. As a result of these interactions and reflections, teachers were able to collectively influence teaching practice across the school. This is a much better way for leaders to influence consistency in schools.

Remember that peer learning benefits both the observer and the observed when undertaken within a spirit of collaboration and mutual learning. No judgements of teaching are made. As the observer, you have the opportunity to watch and enhance your understanding of the complex interactions that take place in the classroom. You can consider the gap between what the planned intended outcomes were and what actually happened. The conversation that takes place afterwards enables you to consider the 'why'. Peer learning enables the observer to observe in a structured way how a teacher uses different strategies when teaching and the impact it has on the students. There may be a specific whole-school focus on a strategy that you are collectively working on, or it may just be an area of practice that the particular teacher has identified for exploration and improvement.

The peer being observed also benefits greatly. As teachers we tend to spend most of our time working in isolation and this is why it is so important to take opportunities for reflection. We make thousands of decisions every day and many of these countless decisions are influenced by our unconscious thinking and tacit knowledge, by our own perceptions and understandings from all the experience we have gained in classrooms. The greatest value of peer learning is the way in which it provides a reflective lens into your classroom and your teaching interactions. Remember that your observer will not make any judgements of your teaching, instead they will share what they have seen, in terms of your practice in relation to the area of focus that you identified. This 'mirroring' will enable you to contribute to the professional dialogue through sharing your own perspective: why did you choose to ask that student that question; why do you think that student didn't understand the task; how well did you explain the learning objective? The dialogue is best placed within a coaching conversation, in which the observer can ask open questions to deliberately enable you to further reflect upon your teaching and interactions. Peer learning is designed to enable you to unpack the complexity of all the interactions that take place in your classroom, in order for you to learn from your current practice to inform future practice, as all good thinking teachers will do.

Peer learning is most effective when the focus is on an agreed specific aspect of practice and isn't too general. Whenever we introduce a new strategy or discuss a piece of research, our teachers will explore it through peer learning and/or lesson studies; these findings are then shared at a whole school level to inform collective future practice.

Lesson study

I cannot emphasise enough how the effectiveness of the activities described in this chapter are dependent upon you working within a team in which there are high levels of mutual trust. As I have discussed earlier, if this is not the case you must search out these opportunities for yourselves with like-minded colleagues. Lesson study is a professional learning tool that has been used effectively in Japan for over a hundred years, and I would describe it as an advanced version of peer learning. It is more effective if it involves a group of teachers, rather than just a pair, and this can make it more challenging to organise. In this section, I will describe how you can use the model of lesson study to support your professional learning and develop your practice to improve outcomes for your students.

As a school, we engaged in peer learning for three years before we even considered lesson study. This meant that when we began to engage in lesson study, we already had in place a positive collaborative learning culture and teachers had become accustomed to visiting each other's classrooms. Lesson study is an extension to peer learning in that it works in tandem with the reflective learning cycle detailed in chapter 3. It provides another avenue through which you can explore your practice in terms of the cycle of planning, teaching and assessment. I had read a series of journal articles on lesson study and I was excited about introducing it to our teaching teams. I was particularly excited about the potential within the lesson study model of groups of teachers coming together to engage in research and observe and critically evaluate what we describe to be the 'research lesson'. I will outline to you the model of lesson study that we implement in our school. This is very important because often when I hear about teachers/leaders describing their engagement in lesson study, what is described to me is not always aligned with my own interpretation. I was also excited about the lesson study model at the time because it seemed so different to my own personal experiences of engagement in professional learning. Where individual teachers feel a sense of dread when being observed by a 'senior leader', the thought of a group of teachers observing you teach may, at first glance, appear to be a horrifying prospect! A strong culture of collaboration and high trust is required to overcome this and that is why I continue to emphasise this throughout the book.

The overall premise of lesson study is for a group of teachers to come together to collaboratively plan a lesson and to observe one member of the team teaching it. We always ensure that the lesson study is research informed. By research informed, we mean ensuring that all members engage with a piece of research to inform their thinking and planning. Examples may include reading research on identified topics, e.g. assessment for learning, dialogic teaching, developing creativity and critical thinking, metacognition. We ensure that there is a minimum of three people involved and usually the group is bigger. A bigger group will work well, as long as all members are equally committed and involved. Reflective practice, action research, peer learning and lesson study are essential components of the 'Thinking Teacher Toolkit', as they all require involvement in reflective cycles of professional learning. Lesson study involves a cycle of plan, observe, reflect, action, repeat.

I will detail the cycle of lesson study through a real-life example that I participated in. I was part of a group of five year 6 teachers who were looking to plan a series of lessons to develop our students' understanding of the relationship between fractions, decimals and percentages. This was a relatively new experience for us in terms of the topic because the mathematics curriculum had been adapted that year and year 6 students were now expected to have a more advanced understanding of calculation of fractions. Teachers were having to teach topics that they hadn't taught before. It was also the first time that we had engaged as a group in lesson study, so we took time to carefully consider the structure. I wanted to adhere as much as possible to the original Japanese model for lesson study and we were very deliberate in describing the planned lesson as a 'research lesson'. We wanted to emphasise the fact that we were expected to take creative risks, to innovate, to experiment in a journey of learning and discovery.

The first step was for us to come together as a group to share and explore our current understanding of the teaching of fractions. This included discussing our own experiences of learning maths/fractions as students ourselves and how these experiences potentially impact upon our own teaching of the subject/topic. We took the opportunity to look at some research on the effective teaching of maths in terms of pedagogic content knowledge, and we decided to focus specifically on our use of questioning to enable our students to reflect more deeply upon how they approached mathematical problems. We also considered Vygotsky's (Yasmitsky, 2018) 'zone of proximal development' and how to ensure that we weren't overloading our students with too much information or moving them on too quickly. This type of collaborative professional dialogue is crucial, and the greatest impediment to it in schools is the availability of 'time'. As a school, we commit to enabling our teachers to engage in collaborative planning/lesson study. If you are having to organise this for yourselves, ensure that you allow sufficient time at this planning stage.

Following the discussion, we planned a single lesson together. We established our enquiry question, which was about the use of questioning to support the effective teaching of calculation skills in fractions. We then planned the lesson, including both teacher questions and the learning activities that we wanted our students to engage in. We also predicted what we believed would be the impact of these planned activities on the students' learning (at both a group and individual level) and how we would assess this. This is what makes lesson study such a powerful and valuable professional learning activity – very rarely would we get the opportunity to engage in so much collective thought and reflection when planning a single lesson. We selected the teacher within the group (we chose the teacher who was the least confident in the teaching of fractions/maths) and each of the four observers were assigned a group of students that they would focus on. Similar to peer learning, you need a clear structure to the process, and it is important that observers remain disciplined and focus solely on the student(s) that they have been assigned to focus on.

The next stage is for the participants to teach/observe the lesson. As an observer, I found it really useful to focus in on a small group of students and to provide a reflective lens on their experiences/interactions/ learning. I made sure that I questioned each student both during as well as at the end of the lesson to ensure that I had a clear understanding of the impact of the teacher on their engagement and learning. As soon as possible after the lesson, it is important for the group to come together to reflect upon the impact of each activity/part of the lesson on the students' learning and how closely this was related to what we expected to see and if not, why? I remember this to be quite a long but very powerful collaborative professional learning conversation.

As mentioned earlier, the biggest challenge to the implementation of lesson study is time. However, I would urge you to take every opportunity possible to participate in lesson study because it is such a powerful model for professional learning. I noticed that there were both formal and informal positive outcomes from our engagement in lesson study. Firstly, we all adapted our teaching of fractions as a consequence. At the end of the year, this cohort of students achieved some of the highest outcomes in maths within our local authority, and question level analysis demonstrated that they scored particularly high for questions in the arithmetic test that involved calculations of fractions. Informally, the levels of challenge and trust within the collaborative working of this particular group had grown considerably. We continued to take informal opportunities to engage in collaborative dialogue about the impact of our teaching on our students, particularly in maths. We tended to look for each other at the beginning and end of the school day and during transitions to informally discuss our planning/teaching/reflections. I'm sure that this had a powerful, positive impact on us as practitioners, and even more importantly, on our students' learning. I'm so confident about the value of lesson study that I have since taught individual lessons in the school hall, with up to 60 education professionals from across the UK and Europe watching! As I'm sure you have realised from reading this section, I am a big fan.

Appreciative inquiry

The aim for me in writing this book is to support the development of happy, confident teachers. Confidence comes from understanding and knowing your craft. Happiness comes from working in a way that is aligned with your values and seeing and feeling that what you are doing in your work is really making a difference. I mentioned in chapter 3 the value of engagement in coaching as the most powerful ongoing professional learning activity that I engage in. Coaching, reflective practice, action research, peer learning and lesson study are all complementary and interrelated professional learning activities. In this section, I will share my understanding of appreciative inquiry that is a form of coaching. It is as important to know and be confident in what you are doing well in the classroom as it is on knowing what is not going well and what you need to develop. Appreciative inquiry is designed to enable you to do exactly that!

Appreciative inquiry is usually used by educators at a school leadership level, to enable them to come together to identify what is working well or going right, rather than focusing on what is going wrong. I think it is also a very useful reflective tool to use at an individual level and a very good form of practice to engage in as you are developing as a teacher. As an individual teacher, you can use appreciative inquiry to develop a personal strategic vision for your classroom. You can also use it within teams that you are part of to inform collective practice. I suggest that you use appreciative inquiry to identify the best of your own practice as well as the best practice that you see around you. The fact that it is such a positive approach makes it both engaging and very powerful. Appreciative inquiry invites you to take time and space out of your classroom to explore the strengths and successes that currently exist, both internally in your own classroom and externally in your school and beyond.

Appreciative inquiry was developed in the mid-1980s by David Cooperrider at Case Western Reserve University, and Suresh Srivastva, at Weatherhead School of Management. They viewed it to be an alternative positive-focused model to view challenges within business organisations. I was introduced to it during a coaching session when I was developing as a leader, and I believe it has influenced both my approach to teaching in the classroom as well as leadership at school and system level. Whether at individual, team or system level, a typical design for appreciative inquiry involves four stages. I would ask you to consider the process and take the opportunity to trial it within your own setting.

1. Discovery

At the discovery stage, you are simply focusing on positivity as the focus of your inquiry. You take the opportunity to identify the best of what you see in your own classroom and take time to really identify what is going well in your classroom and analyse the factors that are enabling these successes. What are the best examples of teaching that you have seen or read about? What element of great practice can you identify and what components enable these successes to happen in the classroom?

2. Dream

This is the stage when, following the positive inquiry that you have engaged in, you deliberately use the findings to create a vision for your future classroom. It is really important that you take time at this visionary stage to make this vision as real and compelling as possible. I hope that there is a clear thread through this book, of detailing the importance of how we align our values with our actions. What type of teacher do you want to be and what do you need to do to get there? You may decide at the dream stage that you need to undertake further exploration/observation in order to identify which element of your practice that you want to develop first as you move towards your future vision. What new ideas would you like to bring forward into your future?

3. Design

At this stage, you use the best of what you have seen to design the strategies that you will decide to take forward into your practice. I hope you will see that the development of a thinking teacher takes time, starting with the mindset, through the development of reflective practice and the use of the range of strategies described in this book. Appreciative inquiry is something that will enable you to continue to develop throughout your career. The design stage is the opportunity for you to think creatively to determine what you will do to move forward in your practice.

4. Destiny

This is the stage at which you put your strategies into action. Following the design stage, you will have identified clear elements of your practice that you wish to innovate with. The purpose of this is to enable you to move towards the teacher you want to be according to all that you have learned from inquiry into the best that you have seen in your own practice and beyond.

Whenever I undertake appreciative inquiry with teachers at my school, teachers find it a positive and enriching form of reflective thinking. I think it is particularly valuable for teachers who can very easily become entrenched in focusing on what is not working well. It snaps us out of this mindset to encourage us to take time to equally consider what is working well. Remember that appreciation is about recognising the best in yourself as well as the people and the world around us. Consider a school as an ecosystem in which appreciative inquiry draws on the strengths of both yourself, your team and the organisation as a whole. By taking regular opportunities to identify strengths, you are able to continually build upon them within a constant cycle of innovation and improvement. Inquiry is important because it encourages you to ask questions of yourself and those around you and to learn from each other.

Creativity

I hadn't planned on writing this section but having just introduced you to appreciative inquiry, I've realised how important it is for thinking teachers to be able to think creatively. I also think it is an underutilised skill amongst teachers in our schools because we often have a distorted view of what creativity and creative thinking actually is. As thinking teachers, we need to both think creatively ourselves and develop classrooms that enable our students to equally think creatively too.

I have discussed the need to focus on effort rather than ability with your students and the importance of celebrating and learning from our mistakes and misconceptions. This is the starting point for creative thinking. I think we have an unhelpful interpretation of creativity in western thinking, in terms of the 'lightbulb' moment or our definition of 'genius'. Too often, creativity is associated with ability rather than effort. We have this image of Isaac Newton discovering gravity after an apple fell on his head, or great thinkers like Einstein that we consider to be geniuses. Well, I can guarantee that Newton did not discover and define gravity in a single moment – I imagine that it would have been a theory that he, amongst others, had been working on for many years. I believe that creativity comes from successive failures and our ability to learn from these successive failures to innovate and improve. I will illustrate this with an example.

I was told this story and although I cannot verify if it is actually true, I will share it with you anyway. It takes place in a pottery class during an evening course in an adult education centre with a single teacher and

20 students. At the end of this particular session, the teacher realises that there were ten students who were doing very well in their learning, whilst there were ten students who had been unsuccessful and had fallen behind. She decided to set some differentiated homework for each of the two groups. For the 'advanced' group she asked them to concentrate on making a single vase at home and to make it as good as they possibly could. For the second group, she told them not to worry about the design of the vases at all. Instead, she told them just to practice making as many vases as they possibly could, in order to improve their basic skills. One group went home that evening feeling quite pleased with themselves and their progress, whilst the other left feeling slightly deflated and questioning their motivation to continue with the course.

Fast forward to the next week and the 'successful' group returned with their single vases, while the other group returned with two large shopping bags filled with their multiple vases. My simple question to you at this point is to ask you to consider which group do you think managed to produce the best vase?

Well, I can tell you it was the students in the latter group, simply through the understanding that creativity and improvement come through successive failures. The first group made a decent individual vase in relation to their current knowledge and understanding, but their knowledge and skills had not progressed significantly more than their performance in the previous session. Whereas for the second group, the practice of continually making vase after vase, meant that they were engaging in a cycle of continual rehearsal, practicing, sharpening and refining. Each time they made another vase, they learned from the mistakes that they had made previously. They could see the improvements that were being made and were motivated and engaged to think creatively and continually improve.

A thinking teacher must think creatively and see mistakes as powerful learning opportunities. To think creatively, consider divergent thinking. Divergent thinking focuses on two key areas. Firstly, you are encouraged to think of as many ideas as you possibly can. So, when considering your practice, you think of as many different things that you could possibly do. At this stage it is just as important to reject ideas because the second thing you do is identify a new original idea. By identifying as many divergent solutions as possible, the argument is that you are more likely to arrive at the novel idea that you choose to implement. Divergent thinking is essential to thinking teachers because it allows you to generate multiple ideas in order to generate innovative and novel solutions to your practice.

I have discussed creative thinking here because as thinking teachers, I am expecting you to continually open up your practice to scrutiny. Through reflective practice, you will develop an authentic and multi-layered understanding of what is going in your classroom and why. Creative thinking is essential for you to build upon these reflections in order to enhance your knowledge and understanding to further develop your practice. In the same way that you are committed to opening up your practice, you will be equally committed in identifying alternative practices and solutions, through the professional learning strategies I have shared with you. In this way, you are able to identify a range of alternative strategies, and this will support you in arriving at novel solutions. This process requires critical and creative thinking. By engaging in this way and learning from successive failures yourself, you are also more likely to design learning activities for your students that will support the development of their critical and creative thinking too.

Summary

In this chapter we have explored the activities that will support your development as thinking teachers. All the activities detailed: action research, peer learning, lesson study and appreciative inquiry, are designed to support you in your engagement in reflective practice. Within the schools I lead, I aim to make it as easy as possible for teachers to participate, and remember that you don't have to undertake a master's degree to participate in action research. Consider ways in which you can incorporate the reflective cycle of action research into your current practice. Do not aim to engage in all these activities straight away and I would suggest a graduated approach. Consider the opportunities currently available for you to undertake peer learning and action research. Once these have become established within your teaching practice, you can proceed to lesson study and appreciative inquiry.

Remember that the ultimate aim is for you to develop your practice and to develop into an empowered and confident teacher. These activities will support you in doing that.

Relevant reading

Black, P. J. and Wiliam, D. (1998) Inside the Black Box. London: King's College, School of Education.

Billet, S. (2006) 'Constituting the workplace curriculum', *Journal of Curriculum Studies* 38 (1) pp. 31-48.

British Educational; Research Association [BERA] (2014). *The Role of Research in Teacher Education: Reviewing the Evidence.* Interim Report of the BERA-RSA Inquiry. London: BERA.

Cordingley, P., Higgins, S., Greany, T., Buckler, N., Coles-Jordan, D., Crisp, R., Saunders, L. and Coe, R. (2015) Developing great teaching: lessons from the international reviews into effective professional development. Teacher Development Trust.

Elliot, J. (2007) 'Assessing the quality of action research', *Research Papers in Education* 22 (2) pp. 229-246.

General Teaching Council for England [GTCE] (2007) *Making CPD better: bringing together research about CPD.* London: GTCE.

Kemmis, S. (2010) What is to be done? The place of action research. *Educational Action Research.* 18 (4) pp. 417-427.

Lomax, P. (2002) Action Research. In Coleman, M. and Briggs, A.R. J. (eds) *Research Methods in Educational Leadership and Management* London: Paul Chapman Publishing, pp. 122-140.

McNiff, J. and Whitehead, J. (2005) *Action Research for teachers: a practical guide.* London: David Fulton.

Mills, G. E. (2003) *Action Research. A Guide for the Teacher Researcher,* 2nd ed. New Jersey: Pearson Education Ltd.

Saunders, L. (2007) *Supporting Teachers' Engagement in and with Research.* London: TLRP.

Somekh, B. (1998) 'The contribution of action research to development in social endeavours: a position paper on action research methodology'. *British Educational Research Journal.* 22 (3) pp. 339-355.

Stenhouse, L. (1975) *An introduction to curriculum research and development.* London: Heinemann.

Yasnitsky, A. (2018) *Vygotsky. An Intellectual Biography.* London: Routledge.

Reflective questions

1. Which of the activities discussed in this chapter are you most motivated to engage in?

2. What opportunities do you currently have to engage in action research?

3. Are there colleagues who can support you in engaging with peer learning?

4. How do you plan to design opportunities for engagement in the activities detailed in this chapter?

5. How do you plan to implement these activities into your practice over the next three years and what do you think the impact will be?

Chapter 5

Strategies for Thinking Teachers

How to teach?

Throughout this book so far, I've shared ways in which you can engage in reflection to develop your practice. When building and developing a school and a positive culture for learning, I encourage all teachers to engage in reflective practice through peer learning, action research, lesson study and appreciative inquiry. I encourage all teachers and create opportunities for them to participate in collaborative professional dialogue. It is equally important for us to consider the topics that we will be focusing on within this dialogue and in this chapter I will discuss the pedagogical teaching strategies that I believe to be important in our development as thinking teachers. It is essential that, as thinking teachers, we are also nurturing the development of thinking students. There are specific aspects of teaching pedagogies that we enable teachers to learn about, as well as a specific order that we follow. I have done this in each of the three schools that I have led.

First, we enable our teachers to have a secure understanding of assessment for learning strategies, starting with an exploration of the work of Black and Wiliam (1998). We then use this research as a base for us to explore dialogic teaching (Alexander, 2017) – some people refer to dialogic teaching as talk for learning or oracy. Once these strategies have become established components of our practice, we explore the development of metacognition with our students. My aim in your development as thinking teachers is to use the reflective practice activities detailed earlier to explore and design how to teach in a way that empowers your students to become creative, independent and critical thinkers.

Assessment for learning

The purpose for you to engage in reflective professional learning activities is to develop your knowledge, confidence and practice. The topics I detail in this chapter are designed to enable you to develop your understanding of the craft of teaching and to influence what you actually do as a teacher. The success of a thinking teacher is judged in terms of your impact on the outcomes of your students. Crucially, this means every individual student that you teach, not just the majority. Assessment for learning is fundamentally about understanding exactly where your students are currently at, which will then influence exactly what you do in the classroom. The key is to continually challenge your students in their thinking and learning, in each lesson you teach, taking into account their current starting points to move them forward. Only by deeply understanding where they currently are (assessment), can we move them on (for learning). I would also argue that in many classrooms, there is an insufficient focus on using strategies effectively to ascertain students' current thinking and learning.

At each school that I have led, I've used collaborative action research to enable teachers to take the time to explore assessment for learning strategies. I explain that assessment for learning (AfL) is an area of practice that we can continually explore and develop. AfL is not just about developing a student's current knowledge, it is also about developing their 'learning powers' and capacity to improve for themselves. The aim is for them to become more active in their learning and essentially, to become thinking students. I have detailed two definitions of AfL:

'The process of seeking and interpreting evidence for use by learners and their teachers to decide where their learners are in their learning, where they need to go to next and how best to get there' (Assessment Reform Group, 2002).

'AfL is an approach to teaching and learning that creates feedback which is then used to improve student performance. Students become more involved in the learning process and from this gain confidence in what they are expected to learn and to what standard' (Cambridge Assessment International Education, 2022).

At a basic level, everything that you say or do in the classroom should relate to AfL. It is about considering where a child is currently at and to plan questioning/tasks/activities to enable their progress. In chapter 2, I discussed the importance of developing the right conditions for learning. These conditions are critical in providing an environment in which our students feel confident to share their thinking, learning and misconceptions. As thinking teachers, AfL will be integrated throughout your practice and can be adapted to suit the age range of the students you are teaching. AfL includes both formative assessment (questioning, feedback, learning intentions, success criteria, peer and self-assessment) and summative assessment (tests, exams, essays), as long as these activities are used to inform your teaching and impact upon students' learning.

I will outline strategies that you can use in the classroom to develop AfL and by utilising these strategies, we can increase the confidence of our students. We often talk about the building of learning powers at our school. An alternative is to discuss the building of self-efficacy in our students. In the same way that becoming thinking teachers is about building your own confidence and self-efficacy, AfL helps build the confidence and self-efficacy of our thinking students. Self-efficacy is about enabling our students to have the self-belief that through sufficient effort and the implementation of learning strategies, they can improve in their learning/performance.

The easiest way that I find to define AfL is the use of assessment of students to identify exactly where they are currently at in their learning. And to then use this information to design learning activities that take into account what they currently know yet challenges them sufficiently to move them progressively on in their learning. I would describe this as the 'sweet spot' for learning. Anything that is too 'challenging' for the student will be demoralising. Anything that is too 'easy' will be demotivating.

1. Planning

AfL should be considered at the planning stage, particularly in terms of your learning intentions and success criteria. Take time to ensure that your students understand the purpose of their learning and why. Plan your learning intentions to effectively take into account prior learning and to make clear to students what they are learning. Your learning intentions will tell your students what they are going to learn and the activities you design will determine how they will learn this. Remember that we are consciously aiming to build our students' confidence and self-efficacy. We do this by involving our students in their learning by stating, and where possible, involving them in co-constructing the success criteria. We ask our students the following three questions when we are establishing success criteria:

1. How will you tell whether the product you create is good?
2. How will you tell if the process you adopt is good?
3. How do you intend to do the best you can in this learning?

Teachers are asked to consider these questions for themselves when they collaboratively plan the learning activities. John Hattie (2012) has discussed how this can make student understanding and knowledge more visible. By establishing success criteria, students are given a clear understanding of what excellence looks like and what they need to do to get there and meet the learning intentions.

2. Questioning

Developing effective practice in AfL takes time and that is exactly what we give our teachers. Opportunities to collaborate with colleagues to trial and experiment with AfL strategies in their classrooms, particularly in terms of questioning, is essential. Only by experimenting and reflecting over time will these questioning strategies become part of your embedded and natural teaching practice. I have provided example strategies that will support your AfL practice:

- **Thinking time.** Think about how much time you give your students after asking your question before taking your answer. Articulate to your students that you have asked a question and that you are providing thinking time in order for every student to have the opportunity to formulate a response. Don't just respond to the first hand up and instead give everybody the opportunity to think about formulating an answer before you select a child to respond.

- **No hands up.** As you are giving thinking time, you are expecting every student to formulate a response, but you do not need your students to put their hands up and will instead choose a student at random. This encourages every student to engage and every student to be thinking. As time goes by, your choices won't be made at random. Instead, you'll be selecting students in order to support your knowledge of their current understanding. You can support this approach by asking students to record their responses on a white board or tablet. This will immediately give you feedback about each student's current understanding/ misconceptions and this will inform your next steps.

- **Wider engagement.** Following the response that you have received, you can involve the wider class and, simultaneously, assess the collective understanding in the room. You can ask the class to put their hands up if they agree with the response or not? Who agrees? Who disagrees? Why?

- **Question stems.** Employ question stems that provide wider responses? These questions are often described as open, rather than closed questions, e.g. why does . . . ? What if . . . ? How would you . . . ? Can you explain . . . ?

- **Use of misconceptions.** Use misconceptions as important launching points for learning. Once you have detailed the learning intentions and the success criteria, ask your students to consider what the potential barriers may be to them achieving success. Begin your lesson with the potential barriers and misconceptions. For example, rather than giving students ten division questions to complete, give them a completed set of ten to mark instead. Ask them to identify the five incorrect answers and to define the misconceptions that caused the student to get those questions wrong.

3. Student dialogue

I will discuss the value of dialogic teaching in more detail in the next section. At this stage just consider the extent to which you use AfL to support student dialogue. For a thinking teacher, include time in your lessons for paired and group discussions and plan for opportunities to summarise and link student learning through mini reviews. Partner talk and group discussions give time and space for your students to consider more deeply their thinking and understanding. You just need to make it very clear what your expectations are and the purpose of the dialogue. Keep it focused. The role of the thinking teacher following such discussions is to summarise the learning for the wider group. You can articulate to the class what you have heard and how this relates to the learning intentions and your students' efforts in meeting the success criteria.

4. Feedback

Feedback relates to the example mentioned, in terms of what you say to your students – at an individual, group and class level – to move them on in their learning. It is important that you listen actively to your students and ensure that the feedback you provide relates directly to the learning intentions and success criteria and is based on your understanding of each student and their particular learning needs, current knowledge and development. It is essential for you, as a thinking teacher, to ensure that your feedback is both sensitive and constructive. As mentioned earlier, I don't believe that any feedback is neutral, it either has a positive or negative effect. Through your feedback, you want to develop your students' knowledge, skills, self-motivation and self-efficacy as learners.

Feedback does not work one way (teacher to student) but is designed to prompt a dialogue. Feedback provides the glue between your teaching and your students' learning and is the process in which students join their teachers to discuss where they currently are at in their learning, where they need to get to next, and how best to get there. I believe verbal feedback to be more powerful than written feedback, so thinking teachers are very active in the classroom, taking every opportunity possible during whole class teaching, group work and independent study, to provide evaluative and constructive feedback to their students. Remember when we discussed evaluative praise in chapter two? Ensure that your feedback makes clear what your students have done well and why, and what they need to do next to continue to improve. Remember that the aim is to build your students' own self-reflection and self-efficacy. Success breeds success, and the more your students can understand what they're doing well, the more motivated they will be to continue to improve. Effective feedback must relate closely to the clearly defined learning intentions and success criteria.

5. Self and peer assessment

Take as many opportunities as possible to enable your students to engage in self and peer assessment. If this is something your students are not familiar with, focus on developing self-assessment first. If you have clear learning intentions and your students have been involved in discussing and co-constructing the success criteria, then self-assessment is a natural next step. This will support your students in taking responsibility and developing their independent learning skills. Give your students opportunities to set targets for themselves and understand what they need to do to improve. Students need self-assessment opportunities to evaluate their success against clear success criteria. This will enable them to identify the improvements they need to make. By engaging in self-assessment, self-evaluation and reflection, these thinking students will develop a deeper understanding of themselves as individual learners. This will also link closely to the development of metacognition, and I will discuss this in further detail later in this chapter.

You will adopt the same principles when undertaking peer assessment, where students become the teacher in providing feedback for each other. You need to set clear instructions for peer assessment, and it needs to be conducted within a culture of mutual respect. Each student assesses their peer's work, according to the success criteria, and will make judgements and highlight areas and provide ideas for improvement. Both students will benefit because, through participating within a collaborative feedback dialogue, both will develop an enhanced knowledge of the components of a successful piece of work.

6. Time

I hope you can see that the development of assessment for learning relates very closely to the development of effective conditions for learning that we discussed in chapter 2. Every component that I discuss in this book is complementary and interrelated in the development of a very powerful learning-oriented classroom culture. You will develop learners in your classroom that are actively engaged rather than passive recipients of knowledge. Consider the current learning environment in your school and the extent to which it supports this culture. Some of the barriers to the effective implementation of AfL are caused by teachers who are not used to working in this way. Remember that, as thinking teachers, we are actively committed to the development of motivated, independent, creative and critical thinkers.

There can be an over emphasis on summative assessment in some classrooms. This section has been about emphasising active in-the-moment assessment for learning, rather than assessment of learning. Remember that I said that the development of AfL requires experimentation and learning over time, and many teachers are not given the professional learning opportunities or the time to experiment. Time is crucial for you to embed AfL practices in your classroom. As discussed previously, when starting at a new school, I provide opportunities for every teacher to engage in collaborative action research to explore AfL. I've provided some of the feedback from those teachers:

'My knowledge and understanding of AfL has been reinforced through sharing and discussing experiences with colleagues and peer learning observations. These experiences enhanced my understanding on how to use different teaching strategies effectively in class to support my learners to move on to the next steps in their learning'.

'My understanding of AfL has widened from focusing on marking and feedback to considering the wider learning environment. I am now more

aware of the importance of children evaluating their own learning and the need for teachers to give them the tools and language to do this, through modelling and questioning. The AfL focus has also given me the opportunity to explore my beliefs about the ethos of the classroom, how children perceive themselves as learners and the impact this has on their learning'.

I could provide countless more examples, but I want to emphasise how important reflection time is to the development of AfL, as one teacher demonstrates:

'*Because I spend more time reflecting on my own learning, the process seems to grow more organically. I feel as if there is always something I need to add to my teaching in order to improve. This willingness to improve derived from the new approach creates pockets of time and frees the mind of unwanted clutter'.*

Dialogic teaching

As thinking teachers, we have created a culture in our classroom which is underpinned by powerful conditions for learning. We have developed this environment further through the implementation of really effective assessment for learning strategies. The next steps are to develop dialogic teaching and then metacognition. Let's start with dialogic teaching. In developing AfL, we discussed the importance of actively listening to our students. To be able to listen to our students, we need to provide as many opportunities as possible for our students to talk and to share their thinking. I had always promoted a talk rich environment in my classroom, but it was only when I engaged with Robin Alexander's work on dialogic teaching (2017) I realised how to effectively implement talk for learning and to really see the direct impact that it has on student outcomes.

The term dialogic teaching was developed by Alexander in the early 2000s and, at a very simplistic level, it harnesses the power of talk to stimulate and extend students' thinking and advance their learning and understanding. Every teacher in every school that I have led is supported to use dialogic teaching strategies. One of the schools that I currently lead has been awarded the Mayor of London Schools for Success award for five years in a row (no other school in our local authority has ever achieved this award more than once). This award is given to schools who demonstrate the greatest progress for children who are considered low prior attainers. I don't really bother much about awards, but we are particularly pleased with this award because it demonstrates that our school is having a fantastic impact on those particular students that are potentially most challenged or disadvantaged. I am convinced that all our students make accelerated progress because of our dialogic teaching approach. That is why I believe all thinking teachers should consider this approach and evaluate the extent to which it will enable you to develop thinking students.

The Education Endowment Foundation (2017) defines dialogic teaching as: 'Dialogic teaching aims to improve pupil engagement and attainment by improving the quality of classroom talk. Teachers are trained in strategies that enable pupils to reason, discuss, argue and explain rather than respond, in order to develop higher order thinking and articulacy'.

As thinking teachers, I'm sure that you will see that pupil talk is at the centre of our teaching practice. Again, dialogic teaching is something that you will have to develop over time. It fits in with the philosophy of thinking teachers in that we experiment and trial changes to our practice and we develop and embed dialogic teaching strategies over time.

The concept of dialogic teaching is not a new one and is linked to models of learning that have been widely established in history. It can be linked to Socratic dialogues from Ancient Greece. The Socratic method emphasises the importance of dialogue between teachers and students, with the role of the teacher to provide thought provoking questions in a quest to explore the underlying beliefs that are influencing the students' views and opinions. Students are expected to actively engage by asking questions of their own. The Nobel Prize winning economist Amartya Sen (2005) has argued that dialogism arises from the Indian tradition of learning with the rise of Buddhism. When I first learned about dialogic teaching, I associated it with my experiences of seminars at university. Throughout my history degree, we would have seminars where we engaged in small group discussions with our tutor – debating and sharing opinions and building on the ideas of each other. We were expected to actively engage and argue as opposed to being passive recipients of knowledge. I thought at the time that if it was an effective method of learning for our most talented students, those studying for a degree, why was it not appropriate for 4-year-olds, 11-year-olds, or 16-year-olds? I've seen how effective it can be to support the learning of all the students in the classroom and that is why I'm emphasising it here. I also believe it is a very egalitarian form of teaching and, as thinking teachers, it is essential that we are inclusive in our teaching. Every student needs to feel heard and needs to feel valued. All the strategies that have been discussed so far in this book will support you to develop dialogic teaching.

I discussed the background to many of the dialogic teaching strategies in chapter 2 when I outlined the importance of respecting and valuing all contributions and efforts. Remember that dialogic teaching and learning will not flourish if we haven't laid the foundations in our classroom that will support reflective conditions for learning. The examples I illustrated in chapter 2 included avoiding stopping at the right answer. This will enable the discussion to continue and engage more students in sharing their thinking and ideas. Dialogic teaching is about the teacher facilitating quality talk. I described the importance of moving away from the question-answer and tell routines of traditional teaching. By teaching dialogically, we move our students away from looking for the answer that is in the teacher's head and focusing more on the thinking that is taking place in our students' heads. The AfL strategies detailed earlier are designed to support dialogic teaching and without them in place, your dialogic teaching will not work as well. On the following pages, I have detailed some key strategies for you to trial and experiment with, in line with everything we have already been focusing on through this book.

The first thing to reflect upon as a thinking teacher is to consider the balance in your classroom between pupil talk and teacher talk. I would argue that in most classrooms there is an imbalance towards too much teacher talk. Some would argue that as the expert, the teacher should be talking and sharing their knowledge. However, this exchange alone will not support learning by itself. As a thinking teacher you will have to consider the range of opportunities that you are facilitating to promote quality student talk. Alexander (2017) has made it clear that teachers need to encourage interactions which encourage students to think, and to do so in different ways. Ensure that your questioning invites responses that require more than simple recall. I remember asking one teacher, who was effectively using AfL strategies, that his teaching could improve simply by asking a follow-up question of each response received. For example, when a student responds, ask them why they think that, or how do they know, or how can they prove it. This ensures that your students' answers are justified, followed up and built upon rather than just received. On the following pages, I will present examples of how we can extend our students' contributions. Through our feedback, we ensure that we are not simply encouraging our students but using evaluative praise to lead thinking forward.

In my first term as a headteacher, I enabled all teachers at the school to engage in collaborative action research within their year group teams to explore AfL teaching strategies. This had a transformative impact on their teaching. By engaging in research and collaborative learning over time, they were able to make sustainable quality changes to their practice. We replicated this model in term two to explore dialogic teaching strategies. As a staff team we actively worked on the development of quality student talk because we realised the value of the connection between talking and thinking. Through quality talk, we could improve student outcomes in every subject. Fundamentally, we believed that if we could improve the quality of talk, we could improve the quality of our education. We made the decision that our curriculum would not simply be taught through the delivery of subject knowledge, but that learning could take place at a much deeper level and to enable our students to solve problems, make sense of their experiences and to treat learning as a social, situated activity. Our teachers felt that through dialogic teaching and learning, they were better equipped to assess and understand each student's learning needs and progress and to frame their learning activities accordingly. Following our investigative work in our classrooms, we identified eight key principles that we believed to be essential in developing a dialogic teaching classroom and I've detailed these on the following pages.

1. Ask students how they feel about their learning

Consider your own classroom and the extent to which you ask your students how they feel about their learning. Motivation is central to a student's engagement in learning. Consider for example how quickly children and young people can engage in new technologies in their lives out of school. How quickly children master computer games and can easily beat adults in those computer games. Whilst engaging in these games, these children know that the more they play the game, the more likely they are to learn more about the game and the more likely they are to be successful. In this situation they realise that effort leads to success, and, even more crucially, they are highly motivated to put that effort in. If we relate this to the classroom, we have to teach in a way that enables us to build our students self-motivation. It is not simply our sole responsibility as teachers to motivate each student. More importantly, it is our responsibility to teach in such a way that nurtures and builds our students' own self-motivation to learn. One of the ways we do this is by regularly asking our students how they feel about their learning. We do this because how we feel about the learning experiences we engage in is linked to our intrinsic self-motivation.

Consider the reflective activities I asked you to engage in earlier, in terms of a successful and unsuccessful learning experience. I asked you to carefully consider the social experience and how you felt before, during and after. Take regular opportunities to enable your students to engage in self-reflection as learners. Example questions for you to use include: what do you enjoy learning in school and why? What are you most excited about? What do you find challenging and why? How does that make you feel? How do you feel when you learn something new? I will discuss metacognition in the final section of this chapter but, at this point, I would like you to acknowledge how we can use dialogic teaching strategies to enable students to develop a deeper understanding of themselves as unique learners.

2. Use questioning to encourage students to justify their answers

It is our aim as thinking teachers to enable our students to move away from their typical classroom experiences, characterised by teachers' addiction to the right answer and our students' quest to arrive at it. Again, I'm not arguing against the value of closed questions that invite formal, exact responses. I'm arguing for a greater balance. I am encouraging the use of open-ended questions that will have more than one possible answer. Find and experiment with the optimum balance between open and closed questions in your classroom and consider the extent to which this impacts upon students' engagement in whole class/group discussions. More open-ended questions will encourage more students in your class to contribute and, combined with the range of strategies discussed in this book, we will work towards a more equitable and inclusive classroom where every student is engaged and motivated to contribute. Students will begin to move away from searching for the right answer they believe to be in the teacher's head. Even when I work with large groups of adults, many are afraid to contribute out of fear of saying the wrong answer because they are searching for the right answer that they think is in my head.

Open-ended questions will encourage our students to think more deeply, as well as developing chains of dialogue in which our students are building upon the thoughts and ideas of each other. Example questions include: what do you think? Why do you think that? How do you know? Do you have a reason? How would you explain that to someone who doesn't understand? Can you be sure? Is there another way? Take time to continually refer to these types of questions and reflect upon the impact on all your students. Reflection through peer learning or lesson study will enable you to consider how this aspect of dialogic teaching, through effective questioning, can become part of your daily practice.

3. Promote an active and dynamic balance between student talk and teacher talk

It is the aim of the thinking teacher to develop an active classroom where the teacher(s) and students are continually engaged in thinking and dialogue. Throughout the learning experience neither the teacher nor the child is ever passive. I still see classrooms where students are sat at their tables in silence whilst the teacher is sat behind their desk. There is nothing wrong with your students working in silence, but I would expect the teacher to always be active. If students are engaging in silent reading,

I would always make sure that I was doing the same. I would also be silent reading, but I would be sitting at a table with my students, modelling the value of engagement in reading. If there was a desk in my classroom, it would be placed against the wall, simply a table on which I could put my things. I did not want the desk to be seen as a barrier between me and my students. Even if your students are silently completing a test for example, take the opportunity to walk around the classroom and silently evaluate your students' engagement and responses. This will give you very useful information about your students as learners and how well they are able to articulate their learning and share their knowledge and understanding in formal examinations.

In an authentic dialogic classroom, students and teachers are always active. Students are encouraged to be active throughout the learning experience and the teacher will actively and constructively intervene to facilitate and promote their students' engagement. Remember the strategies discussed in chapter 2, including the value of not responding to every student's responses. By not saying anything or giving any feedback, this will encourage your students to think more deeply and provide extended responses. Furthermore, you can facilitate the dialogue by asking peers to respond to each other rather than the teacher. I know how valuable this approach has been to the teachers that I've worked with over many years. They have articulated to me the value in the classroom of extending the dialogue by asking students to give their opinions on the responses of others. This enables your students to build on the ideas of each other rather than waiting passively for the teacher to actively respond to the comments made by each student.

4. Establish your expectations by developing a talk charter

As a teaching team, we couldn't just develop a dialogic classroom through the implementation of dialogic teaching strategies. Or more precisely, we could, but we could develop it even quicker if we deliberately enabled our students to develop the skills to effectively engage in quality talk. The earlier we do this with our students the better, so we teach the rules of quality talk when our students enter reception – aged four years old. Examples include getting our students to listen actively, to wait their turn before speaking, and how to respectfully respond to a comment that they disagree with. Our reception students are taught to use the sentence starters, 'I agree with' and 'I disagree with'. As they develop, they are encouraged to justify these responses. As they get older the students will learn to say, 'I partially agree' with or 'I partially disagree with because. . .'

We decided that the best way to start the year and to reinforce our students' understanding was to co-construct and establish a talk charter in every classroom. The talk charter represents the agreed class rules for promoting quality talk and it can be referred to regularly during your teaching both to positively reinforce good examples of quality talk as well as to highlight when your students have fallen short of the expectations and how this has negatively impacted upon the collaborative classroom dialogue. At the beginning of the year, open up discussions with your students about how and why they feel talk is important to their learning. What skills do they think are required to facilitate high quality talk and dialogue? You can even give the students an interactive group activity through which they can identify and summarise the key skills required to succeed in their learning through talk. Do not underestimate the value of listening! The key findings, through the co-construction between you and your students, are then put on display in your classroom as the talk charter.

5. Build your students' learning powers by making sure you don't scaffold too much

When I work with student teachers or early career teachers, one of the things that I notice is that they often intervene too quickly or are too over-enthusiastic in seeking to help their students. This can often have the opposite effect to its intended purpose. Rather than helping the student, it can inhibit the development of your students' resilience and learning strategies and can make them more reliant upon an adult to support them in their learning. For example, when a child is stuck, we feel that we must support them and scaffold their learning. It is OK to scaffold your students' learning. It is equally OK to respond to your students when they say they are stuck with: 'Good. It's good to be stuck. Keep going and consider alternative ways of looking at the problem. I will come back and check on you in five minutes'. In this situation, the task is clearly challenging and it may be worthwhile to give your students further time to consider alternate ways to approach the learning problem that they are faced with. This may include accessing additional resources or speaking to their peers on their table.

Students need the opportunity to explore and discover new learning for themselves; not just to see the discovery of learning through the lens of listening to or working with their teacher. In the same way that thinking teachers are reflective, your students equally require time and space to consider their learning rather than instantly turning to their teacher for scaffolding. Once they realise the value of this time for deeper reflection, the more they will develop a motivation for self-reflection and their independent learning skills. Thinking teachers allow time, space and support to enable their students to think for themselves how they could solve a problem or what further resources they could access to develop their knowledge and understanding. Through engagement in peer learning and studying audio transcripts of lessons, our teachers realised that they were often too quick to intervene in scaffolding the learning for their students, particularly those that they perceived to be struggling. Consider your own classroom and the extent to which it is the same students that always seem to be struggling and the very same students that are more independent, persistent and resilient. As thinking teachers, it is our aim to empower our students to think for themselves. Consider the interactions you have with your students and the extent to which you are empowering your students to become effective independent learners. Acknowledge that some of our interactions may actually disempower our students and make them more reliant on adult support. When students are given further opportunities to persevere with a challenging piece of learning, in a safe environment, they are more likely to see the value of taking risks and to become more resilient.

6. Value the power of teaching from misconceptions

As discussed in chapter 2, we are aiming to create a culture in which our students can take risks and are unafraid of making mistakes. In addition, we want to encourage them to see the power of using misconceptions as valuable launching pads for learning. As thinking teachers, we will actively plan to use misconceptions to develop all our students' thinking and learning. Through dialogic teaching, we are purposefully giving our students opportunities to identify potential misconceptions that may be developing in their learning and to take time during lessons to explore them. By giving opportunities to consider and discuss these misconceptions during your teaching, you are working towards building a deeper understanding of key concepts for your students. Only when we are consciously aware of potential misconceptions can we arrive at a secure understanding of key aspects of learning.

Take the time to explore your students' individual misconceptions with the class. Not only may other students have similar misconceptions, but just through the process of exploration you are enhancing the understanding of all learners. It is important to consider the extent to which everything we have discussed in this book is interlinked. Your students will only be willing to share and discuss their misconceptions if we have nurtured the conditions for learning that enable our students to feel safe to take risks, make mistakes, articulate those mistakes and learn from them. Remember that we are encouraging the same conditions for learning within our school environment for our thinking teachers. We want our teachers to be working within an environment of safety where they are encouraged to trial changes, take risks, to make mistakes and learn from them. It is the difference between being told something by your teacher and learning it for yourself. The creative process through which we self-assess and discover learning for ourselves will lead to a deeper and more sustainable understanding.

7. Model your own thinking for your students

Take time to model language and critical thinking skills for your students. Every activity that I ask students to engage in during my teaching will also be undertaken by me at the same time. Whether that means a page of arithmetic sums, a piece of creative writing or a science investigation, I will always participate in and complete the very same learning activity. That is because I don't just see myself as the teacher in the classroom, I also see myself as the lead learner. As the lead learner, I will complete the set task and share with my students how I approached the task, what challenges I faced, what thinking I engaged in and how I felt during the task. As students experienced in self and peer assessment, I will invite them to assess the outcomes I've produced as well as my approach, and how this has impacted upon the learning and understanding of all of us. I will invite the students to evaluate my approach to the task and offer advice for my further development as a learner.

I find that by engaging in the task myself, this supports the motivation and engagement of my students. Students genuinely value and enjoy listening to their teacher's approach to an activity and, most significantly, their thinking. As thinking teachers, we want to share our own thoughts to positively influence our students' approaches to their learning. By sharing our own thinking, we are developing a climate in which we equally encourage our students to feel safe to share their thinking too. I will share things that might concern me or worry me when approaching a task. As a teacher, I'm demonstrating to my students that we are all learners. By articulating our thinking and approaches, we are modelling effective approaches to learning for our students. Your students will benefit from listening to your thinking processes and learning strategies. And they will genuinely enjoy seeing the work that you have produced, or, in my case, the not so great art work I produce!

8. Provide developmental verbal feedback to move thinking forward

Remember in chapter 2 how I emphasised the need to ensure that all praise is constructive and evaluative. In a dialogic classroom we ensure that all feedback to our students is positive, constructive, informs our students' thinking and leads it forward. Be very clear to your students in terms of what they've done well in their learning and why. For example, be really specific about why your student's response was well thought out, how it could be further enhanced, what further potential links to learning can be made, where their viewpoints may have arrived from, where that learning has come from and where it can potentially lead to. We really need to articulate for our students what they're doing well and why and how this will support them in their future learning and development.

Metacognition

The final aspect of pedagogy that we will explore in this book is metacognition and how we can develop our students' metacognitive strategies. To get to this point, we've taken time to reflect upon the learning environment that we wish to create and nurture within our classrooms. We have discussed how we wish to develop the right conditions for learning that will enable our students to both succeed and improve, as well as raising their motivation and self-efficacy. Following this, we considered how we can skilfully and effectively use a range of assessment for learning strategies to ensure that each of our students is challenged to move on in their learning, in relation to their individual starting points. Once these structures are intrinsically embedded within our classroom practice, we develop an environment that promotes dialogic teaching. As thinking teachers, we are developing thinking classrooms. We have therefore developed both the conditions and the culture in our classroom that is essential if we are to develop metacognition with our students. In this section, we will consider the strategies we can deploy to help our students develop metacognition.

Metacogition, a bit like when we referred to lesson study, is often talked about in schools but not always well understood. Take a moment now to reflect upon your current understanding of metacognition. What do you currently understand about metacognition and what would you like to learn more about? At a very basic level, metacognition is thinking about thinking. Or even, thinking about learning. The reason that I promote metacognition in the schools that I lead is because it both supports our students' learning in the moment [in terms of each lesson], as well as enabling them to develop a deeper understanding of their own learning processes. Throughout this book we have talked about the importance of developing excellent learning relationships with our students and of empowering our students to develop self-efficacy and a strong understanding of themselves as learners. Some of the students that you teach will have better developed metacognitive skills than others and as thinking teachers, it is our responsibility to enable all students to develop metacognitive skills. It is a tool to unlock your students' effectiveness as learners. Students who have well developed metacognitive skills have an enhanced awareness of their own strengths and weaknesses in their current learning and will have a positive mindset in employing their own strategies to both solve problems and to maintain and enhance their own self-motivation. Metacognition is about each of us developing our understanding of ourselves as learners and considering how we plan, monitor and evaluate the effectiveness of our own learning. Metacognition is therefore central to the skillset of a thinking teacher and our work in the classroom.

By using strategies to develop our students' metacognition, we will actively take opportunities to enable our students to plan, monitor and evaluate the effectiveness of their own learning. We do this in order to empower our children to develop these strategies for themselves. By reflecting upon themselves as learners, they will actively make changes to their own learning behaviours. This will include enabling your students to develop their understanding of both metacognitive knowledge and metacognitive regulation. Metacognitive knowledge refers to what students know about themselves in terms of their own cognitive abilities. For example, I know that I'm very good at remembering dates. I also know that I often have to reread a piece of text for me to develop an effective understanding. What we will do as thinking teachers is give our students knowledge of different strategies that they can use for different tasks. This will allow them to consider which strategies are most appropriate for the challenges that they are facing. They will also draw from their own knowledge of facing similar challenges in the past. Metacognitive regulation refers to what students do about learning. It describes how your students monitor and control their own understanding of the learning process. For example, we want our students to realise for themselves that a particular strategy is not working, and to deploy a different strategy, without always needing to go to the teacher. As thinking teachers, we have emphasised the importance of self-reflection. It must be our aim to equally develop these same skills of self-reflection in the students that we are teaching.

To summarise, I will discuss here the interrelationship between cognition and metacognition and their links to our self-motivation as learners. The way in which we develop our own understanding of cognition and metacognition as learners, as well as our motivators, is key to our self-regulation. Self-regulation, or self-efficacy as we described earlier, is what we are aiming to develop in our students. We want to develop their own learning powers and their self-motivation is absolutely central to that.

Consider cognition as our mental learning powers. These are the powers we use to build our own knowledge and understanding. Examples of cognitive strategies include how we use strategies to remember facts and information. Metacognition is the way in which we evaluate, drive and direct our own learning. Metacognitive strategies are the strategies we use to evaluate and check that the learning powers we are using, such as remembering knowledge, have been successful.

Motivation is essential to this development because it demonstrates the extent to which we actually want to use our cognitive and metacognitive strategies, consistently and effectively applying them to our learning. Consider students that are undertaking GCSEs. They will only engage in independent study and revision throughout year 11 if they are self-motivated and understand that the amount of effort that they put into their revision is directly related to how well they will do in their exams at the end of the year. Put simply, the more that they engage in revision tasks, the better they will become in developing their cognition and metacognition strategies, the better they will become at self-regulation, the more knowledge they will acquire about themselves as learners and their motivators, and the more successful they will become as learners. Hopefully that makes sense, or maybe like me, you may just want to read through that paragraph one more time to deepen your understanding!

Metacognition is about giving your students as many opportunities as possible to engage in tasks that not only develop their knowledge and understanding but also equally enables them to develop a deeper reflective understanding of themselves as learners. This will include lots of repetitive activities that allow your students to develop, rehearse and sharpen their skills. Even as adults and experienced learners, very rarely do we learn something the first time and perfect it. By engaging in learning over time and regularly undertaking tasks/activities, the learning will transfer from our short-term working memory to our long-term memory. We've agreed throughout this book that reflection is key to our development as thinking teachers. I also argue that reflection must be central to the development of our students as thinkers and learners. That is why we need to get our students thinking and reflecting at every stage of the learning process. Students need to reflect upon their learning intentions and the success criteria within each lesson and this will inform how they independently approach a task. They will then need to draw upon their cognitive and metacognitive strategies to monitor and evaluate what they have produced. Similar to the reflective cycles discussed earlier in the book, your students will reflect on the effectiveness of their learning and consider what alternative strategies they may draw upon to improve on their learning in the future.

We also want to ensure that our students take opportunities to reflect during the learning process, not just at the end of it. Therefore, you will need to give opportunities during your lessons for students to reflect on their current effectiveness in the task, and alternative strategies that they may wish to draw upon. This is related to the earlier example shared where Schon (1991) talked about reflection in action as well as reflection on action. Remember that we want to develop thinking teachers and thinking students. I'm expecting you to reflect during your teaching about the effectiveness of the strategies that you are deploying to support and enhance your students learning. Equally, we want to give our students regular opportunities to reflect upon their own learning in 'the moment' and to consider the effectiveness of their strategies and what they may want to do differently during the learning process. We want to, therefore, use opportunities during each lesson for student self-reflection and peer reflection as well as at the end of the learning process. A classroom which has an authentic structure and culture of assessment for learning and dialogic teaching will really support your students' self-reflection and metacognitive development. Even more importantly, this will enhance their self-regulation and self-motivation. Remember that as thinking teachers, we are aiming to develop our students' learning powers and thinking skills in order to support the development of their knowledge.

So, what do we need to do as thinking teachers to develop our students' metacognition? Well, AfL and dialogic teaching will certainly support that. With clear learning intentions and success criteria, your students will be able to plan, monitor and evaluate their own learning. Through dialogic teaching, your students will be given regular opportunities to discuss and share their own learning and thinking and to learn from and build upon the ideas of others. We are encouraging our students to continually self-reflect and you may want to pause and consider what opportunities you give for your students to record these reflections. We use a reciprocal reading model at our school in which children are placed in small mixed attaining groups to discuss a text. We do this to develop our students' comprehension skills, as well as their motivation to engage in reading. We give the students opportunities to make predictions and to summarise their understanding. These strategies will support reflection. Do not underestimate the value of modelling and sharing your own thinking as a learner for your students. Remember that I highlighted that some of your students may develop their metacognitive skills more naturally. These students are then described as high ability or higher attaining. By modelling your own thinking and sharing your own metacognitive strategies, you are scaffolding the development of these strategies for all your students.

All the strategies that I have shared in this book are not strategies that can simply be taken off the shelf and seamlessly implemented into your classroom teaching the following day. They are to be developed over time within a culture of ongoing self-reflection as a teacher. They are interrelated and supportive of each other and require a commitment to a culture of inclusive learning for all. It is my job as a school leader to support teachers to develop their metacognitive teaching strategies over time and I always begin by giving them a range of metacognitive questions that they can then use within their classroom. The intention is for teachers to begin to introduce these questions into their teaching and consider the extent to which they are empowering their students as learners.

Example questions will include:

What can you do today that you couldn't do last week?

How do you know when you have learned something?

Can you prove it?

Can you show me your understanding in a different way?

Why did you choose to do it that way?

Why did you change your mind?

What do you need to remember?

What do you need to do to help you?

What was the tricky bit?

What things really made you think today?

What were you proud of today?

How do you feel when you learn something new?

How do you feel when it gets tricky?

Why do you think you were successful today?

Summary

Through the course of this book, it has been my aim to equip you with the skills to be an effective thinking teacher. In this chapter, I have focused on strategies that you will implement and reflect upon in your classrooms. As thinking teachers, it is our aim to develop thinking students. Students who have the skills to self-reflect and to engage in their learning as independently as possible. We want them to be self-motivated to learn and to understand themselves as learners. Consequently, we must nurture and promote a classroom climate that allows our students to question, reflect and flourish. This chapter has presented strategies that will enable you to develop both the structures and culture that will provide an inclusive climate where all students can thrive.

We discussed the importance of assessment for learning, enabling us to clearly identify where our students are currently at and how to sufficiently challenge them in each lesson to move them on in their thinking and learning. We discussed the need to create a culture where there is an effective balance between student talk and teacher talk. Dialogic teaching strategies were shared to enable us to develop an equitable classroom where all students have a voice and there are sufficient opportunities to build upon the thinking of their peers and to learn from each other. Finally, we considered the value of metacognitive strategies that enable us to develop our students' learning powers. All these strategies are interrelated and interdependent and are developed by thinking teachers over time. By doing this, we are purposefully developing thinking students within our thinking classrooms.

Relevant reading

Alexander, R. J. (2017) *Towards dialogic teaching: rethinking classroom talk.* 5th ed. York: Dialogos.

Assessment Reform Group (2002) Assessment for Learning: 10 principles. Research-based principles to guide classroom practice.

Black, P. J. and Wiliam, D. (1998) Inside the Black Box. London: King's College, School of Education.

Cambridge International (no date) 'Getting started with...', bit.ly/2mXZicc.

Education Endowment Foundation (2017) Dialogic Teaching. Cambridge Primary Review Trust & York University.

Hattie, J. (2012) Visible learning for teachers. Abingdon: Routledge.

Schon, D. (1991) *The Reflective Practitioner – how professionals think in action.* Aldershot: Ashgate.

Sen, A. (2005) The Argumentative Indian: Writings on Indian History, Culture and Identity. London: Allen Lane Books.

Reflective questions

1. How would you describe the current learning environment in your classroom in relation to AfL, dialogic teaching and metacognition?

2. Is there a shared understanding across your school of expectations for teaching and learning?

3. What aspect of the strategies shared in this chapter would you most like to trial next in your classroom?

4. Consider the students who you are currently teaching in terms of their own self-reflection and understanding of themselves as learners.

5. Are there students that you are currently working with that have effective metacognitive strategies in place? How did they develop these and how do the strategies impact upon their learning in your classroom?

6. What is your plan for the development of your teaching over the next six/twelve months? Consider writing this plan in a reflective journal.

Chapter 6
Conclusions

I wrote this book because I wanted to share the findings of my research and experience in developing thinking teachers within a thinking school. I am genuinely excited about the impact of such teachers on the outcomes of their students – not just academically but also emotionally, socially and personally. There is sufficient evidence to indicate that we need to reconceptualise the role of the teacher to include a specific focus on ongoing professional learning. By developing the skills of thinking teachers, you will develop your own self-motivation and confidence as well as your knowledge and practice. This will enable you to navigate the choppy waters that all teachers face at the start of their careers as well as meet the various challenges you will continue to face throughout your teaching journey. Central to the role of the thinking teacher is reflective practice and continual engagement in deep and meaningful professional learning activities.

I've been concerned throughout my career about the numbers of dedicated and committed practitioners who either struggle in teaching or are forced to leave the profession. At its best I believe teaching provides one of the most enjoyable and rewarding jobs. When writing *The Thinking School*, I acknowledged the importance of school leaders in designing and implementing a climate in which all teachers can continually learn, grow and develop. This book has been aimed at empowering the reader, as an individual teacher, to take charge of your own learning and positively influence the professional learning climate in which you are working. I have argued for a reconceptualisation of the role of the teacher, with reflective practice and engagement in expansive professional learning activities such as peer learning, lesson study and action research, as a prerequisite of this role. As thinking teachers, we will continually engage in reflective practice in an ongoing cycle of learning and improvement of our teaching.

A thinking teacher is unafraid of taking risks to improve their practice. They are research informed and work collaboratively with their peers to reflect upon and improve their teaching. At the beginning of this book, I asked you to consider your 'why', in terms of the values, motivations and dispositions that will influence the type of teacher you choose to become. Teaching is a tough job and the conversations that we have with ourselves will influence the extent to which we both enjoy our job as well as our success. To become a thinking teacher, you must develop the mindset of lifelong learning. We accept that we can never become the perfect teacher. We also do not beat ourselves up when we make mistakes or teach lessons that don't go as planned. What we do is reflect during and after each lesson to identify areas for development. We also ensure that we build excellent learning relationships with our students and colleagues.

I explained the need for you to take responsibility by positively influencing the learning environment in which you are working. Returning to the OECD report (2016) on the teaching profession discussed in chapter 3, researchers described how teaching and learning approaches have remained the same despite constant changes to conceptions of pupil learning and the skills required for students to contribute effectively to society. They argued that three key ingredients are required to create a responsive 21st century school:

1. Teachers who are confident in their ability to teach.
2. Teachers' willingness to innovate.
3. Strong school leaders who establish the conditions in their school that enable the former two ingredients to flourish.

Ball (2013) rightly argues that education requires a new kind of informed teacher who is committed to collaborative learning. I think that what they are both arguing for is the development of thinking teachers. Through ongoing reflection and engagement in research, thinking teachers become more knowledgeable about effective teaching strategies and how to implement them in their teaching. They can personalise their approaches to ensure that every student learns and succeeds, and only the best teachers can do this. This is where teacher confidence comes from. Through active experimentation and reflection, we become more confident about our skill set and how to use these skills in our teaching. We are collaborative with our students and our colleagues and we are innovative and open to new ideas. We are continually engaging in research and trialling changes to our practice.

I have highlighted that there will be challenges if you are working in an environment in which this type of innovation is not supported or encouraged. However, I've written this book to enable you to undertake professional learning activities that will support you in the development of your practice. Thinking teachers are learning focused in relation to their own learning and their students' learning. They understand the importance of their own professional learning and how this has a powerful influence on the quality of their students' learning experiences. They also analyse and evaluate every decision they make and every action they take, in terms of its direct positive impact on the learning outcomes of the students they teach.

I've urged you to consider your mindset as a teacher. To take the time to visualise for yourself the type of teacher that you want to be and the type of classroom that you want to create for your students. As thinking teachers, we believe that we can have a transformative impact upon the students that we are teaching. Transformative teaching is about recognising and embracing the powerful impact that we can have on our students, as well as being open to transforming our own practice in order to continually improve. I also asked you to transform your relationship with risk taking. Rather than seeing risks as threatening, we should consider them as essential to our own learning and growth, as well as our students' learning. As thinking teachers, we will set no limitations for our continued development and growth. I've continually highlighted the complexity and challenges that a career in teaching will provide. I urge you to embrace these challenges and to not be overwhelmed by them. Through engagement in research and reflective practice you will overcome the challenges that you face. The professional learning activities described in this book are designed to enable you to become more confident and develop a greater sense of self efficacy as teachers. They will support both your personal wellbeing as a teacher as well as your effectiveness.

Central to the role of a thinking teacher is to engage in reflective practice, and through the book I shared several examples of ways in which you can do this. Action research, peer learning, lesson study, coaching and appreciative inquiry will all provide opportunities for you to purposefully engage in a reflective cycle of learning. These strategies are all complementary and interrelated and will enable you to become more confident and effective in your teaching. I want you to take control of your own professional learning and to believe in your own capacity for self-development. Teaching can be a really rewarding career but also a challenging one. Thinking teachers will both meet these challenges and embrace the rewards. I enjoy being challenged as a teacher and I continually draw upon reflective practice to support me to meet those challenges and to continually improve. I still enjoy every day of teaching, even after more than 20 years, and I continue to engage in reflective research-based practice to improve.

I've also acknowledged through this book that as thinking teachers, we have a responsibility to nurture the development of thinking students. We hold a commitment to develop our students to gain the motivations and skills to be lifelong learners. I detailed the power of assessment for learning, dialogic teaching and metacognition in enabling you to do this. Through a combination of these teaching pedagogies and the reflective practices detailed, you will learn to teach in a way that empowers your students to become knowledgeable, self-motivated, creative, independent critical thinkers. Our education system and our children and young people need thinking teachers.

Relevant reading

Ball, S. J. (2013) *Education, justice and democracy: the struggle over ignorance and opportunity.* London: Centre for Labour and Social Studies.

Schleicher, A. (2015) *Schools for 21st century learners: strong leaders, confident teachers, innovative approaches.* Paris: OECD Publishing.